Transformational
Architecture

Transformational
Architecture

Reshaping Our Lives as Narrative

RON MARTOIA

ZONDERVAN®

ZONDERVAN.com/
AUTHORTRACKER
follow your favorite authors

ZONDERVAN®

Transformational Architecture
Copyright © 2008 by Ron Martoia

This title is also available as a Zondervan ebook.
Visit www.zondervan.com/ebooks.

Requests for information should be addressed to:

Zondervan, *Grand Rapids, Michigan 49530*

Library of Congress Cataloging-in-Publication Data

Martoia, Ron, 1962–
    Transformational architecture : reshaping our lives as narrative / Ron Martoia.
      p. cm.
    ISBN 978-0-310-28769-8 (softcover)
    1. Storytelling — Religious aspects — Christianity. 2. Narrative theology. I. Title.
  BT83.78.M37 2008
  246'.72 — dc22
                                    2008026369

Published in association with the literary agency of Daniel Literary Group, LLC, 1701 Kingsbury Drive, Suite 100, Nashville, TN 37215.

Interior design by Beth Shagene

Printed in the United States of America

08 09 10 11 12 13 14 • 23 22 21 20 19 18 17 16 15 14 13 12 11 10 9 8 7 6 5 4 3 2 1

Ron and Pat Martoia, my parents, were the primary influencers and shapers of my early Christian experience. If it hadn't been for their love, support, and cheerleading, I would have never found my way spiritually or become interested in spiritual conversations and ministry.

Kay O'Malley, my maternal grandma, is one of those praying saints—and while I am tempted to say "old praying saints," she would be on the phone to remind me that *old* is always a relative term, even at eighty-nine years of age. The slow drip of her prayers to God for her grandson is a treasure whose worth only eternity will calculate.

■

To Dad, Mom, and Grandma,
who are indirectly responsible
for the shape and content
of this book

Contents

Acknowledgments

A book such as *Transformational Architecture* is forged in the context of hours of conversations with those who share a similar journey, those who are willing to explore with you unfamiliar terrain and humor your outlandish ideas.

I process thoughts in so many ways. But the greatest clarity for me comes when verbal sparring happens with those who are equally tuned to the material. Joe Lengel is simply an unparalleled conspirator. His breadth of reading and processing capability coupled with his translational skill have made our relationship genuinely symbiotic and rich. Joe, thanks is hardly enough.

I have spent hours with Ted Baird on and off the continent talking about these themes and a lot of other things. His observations and willingness to anticipate potential push-backs and to be a sounding board are invaluable. The rejuvenation that happens among deep friends is what keeps life fresh and creativity bubbling. Deep gratitude and much love, Ted.

Gabe Lyons was willing to let one of the core ideas in this book get airtime in an article that is part of a larger collection known as Fermi Shorts. His willingness to take risks and include me in the conversation is a gift I don't take lightly.

Edgar Cabello and his team at Calvary Temple were willing to host a number of learning conversations when I was in the thick of writing this book. It is impossible when your mind is compiling writing data to not share it in speaking contexts. For all the conversations and the forum you provided for Velocity learning conversations, I am grateful.

Let's have an honest admission: presidents and CEOs do not run their companies, let alone their offices; executive assistants do. During this writing project Nancy Carpenter set up all the learning conversations and "in real life" meetings hosted by Velocityculture, my web/consulting/learning presence on the Web. She and all the other executive assistants are gems who are attempting to run most of the Western hemisphere. I couldn't have done it without you, Nanc.

Angela Scheff has become my most recent educator. I have not only learned an enormous amount from her critical editing skills but also witnessed her gracious delivery and gentle demeanor. I am quite certain this book is better because of your input. Thank you for your investment and encouragement in this project. I appreciate you.

Lastly, I want to thank those who have attended Spiritual Explorations Live, Velocity learning conversations, III:TEXT learning experiences, and speaking events I've been at in the last eighteen months. I think of people like Samurai Jack, Paully, John K, Mark, Tracy, Kristi, Bill and Sandy, Betsy and Clark, Pat and Jamie, Dean and Tasha, Lori, Mitzi, Eric, Julie, Trish, and a host of others. This book has been shaped directly by your interactions and encouragement. The intimacy of learning conversations are incredible venues for the tussle and scuffle that help to form, deform, and eventually re-form ideas. I have experienced deeper shalom and fullness because of your presence in my life.

Let the journey begin, and may our lives be further shaped and formed.

■ Ron
June 2008

Transformational Architecture

"I would just love to find a better way to connect with people when it comes to spiritual things." How many times have I said *that* to myself? How many times have I had people say that to me? If you are a follower of Jesus, if you take his motivational charge in Matthew 28 seriously, if you love him and what he has done in your life, then it is a natural overflow to want to share it with others. The question, of course, is, "How?" My journey into the realm of spiritual conversations, like anyone else's, has had its ups and downs. And having been a local church pastor for nearly two decades honestly didn't qualify me any better than the average person to effectively "share my faith." I experienced the same guilt and frustration as the people I served in learning how to communicate with soccer parents, neighbors, and workout acquaintances at my local gym.

My frustrations at ineffectiveness—my blunderings at getting the conversation started or "waiting for it to organically emerge" —were not just common to me but to every person I knew. I didn't have one personal example in my experience in which the issue of sharing faith seemed to catalyze in natural ways. So what is the deal? What is so hard about this "evangelism" thing (to use the old-school term) that so many of us are ready to give up?

I think the answer is easier and maybe more compelling than we realize. In the last ten years, scores of books have been written to try to answer this question, and my sense is they all have one thing in common: they assume the message we have been communicating is the correct one. The problem, these books contend, is our *method* of inviting. If we could just tweak the way we evangelize, get more relational, or do better apologetics, we would finally have the evangelistic silver bullet.

I believe we can change our methods on a monthly or even daily basis, but if the starting point is wrong, or if the story we are communicating and inviting others to experience is an abbreviated, low-calorie version of the real thing, then we have missed the real issue. Our problem isn't just one of method but of message as well.

When we aren't questioning whether we are telling the right story, we're not questioning the starting point for the story either. This "aha" experience has been life changing for me. I certainly don't believe I have all of this figured out, but I do think I've taken steps in the right direction. When I start the story where God starts the story, which is different from what I learned in seminary evangelism classes, I find that people are genuinely interested in spiritual conversations. Why? God's original architectural plans for human "heart space" designed us with cravings, longings, yearnings, that sit at the intuitive level of our lives. These primal elements, architected deep in the core of our being, drive our desire for transformation. In other words, "evangelism" is really about helping people along in a journey for which they have desire already *built into* them at the center of their hearts.

My evangelistic training was always centered on the need to persuade, convince, and prove how bad sin was and how it was an impediment to the wonderful plan God had in mind. Neither concept ever met with deep resonance or much interest. My training never equipped me to identify what was going on in a person's life or how to identify their yearnings. What I've come to discover is that every human being has these intentionally architected design elements that drive the desire for transformation. As Christ-followers, our role is to help people get conversational airtime.

When we begin to consider these things with our friends, they almost always find instant resonance. How can it be otherwise? God's design was intentional. I want to help us come to grips with these architectural plans God uses. He gives us a lot of hints and clues, but if you're like me, they may be so subterranean we miss them.

Conversations in everyday life often swirl around things such as *meaning* (what am I doing here?), *happiness*, and *wholeness/ brokenness*. Those conversations might not always use that language, but they are happening. What would happen if we began to understand the deepest designs of the human heart and started the conversation there?

While learning old patterns and practices has been hard for me, unlearning stories I was convinced I had all figured out has been even harder. In sharing some of my story, I hope we will not only discover new ways to engage people (hints and clues to approaches) but also unlearn an abbreviated story and learn a sweeping narrative story of what God wants to do in a human life (learning the full message). Unlearning and new learning are never easy.

The Axis Point

In his book *Deep Change*, Robert Quinn observes that people and organisms have only two options—slow death or deep change.[1] For the church of Jesus to make deep change, individuals will need to make deep and profound changes. We live at an axis point of cultural transition, making the need for deep change even more acute. We weren't too effective in the dying modern world, so now we get to see how well we can engage the world of postmodernity.

We face a similar situation to that of two of the great Protestant Reformers who went before us—Martin Luther and John Calvin. What makes their circumstances so instructive is that they, too, lived at a transitional node between eras. For them, it was the transition from the Middle Ages into the modern world. For us, it is the transition from the modern to the postmodern world. For them and for us, the issue is our (in)ability to disembed our Christianity from one dying worldview and reengage it in fresh ways in the new emerging world. We need to learn how Luther and Calvin handled Nicolaus Copernicus and Galileo Galilei.

The prevailing worldview of the day, the cosmology that held sway throughout the Middle Ages, had the earth at the center. This was known as *geocentrism* (*geo* = earth, *centrism* = center). The theologians of the time period, including Luther and Calvin, knew that this had to be the way the world was, because Joshua prayed for the sun to stand still—and it did.[2] In other words, for this text to be correct, Luther and Calvin reasoned, the earth must be at the center, with the sun rotating around it. When the Tuscan physicist and astronomer Galileo Galilei teamed up with the Polish astronomer Nicolaus Copernicus to present their findings, it didn't go over well with the church. Their calculations had the sun situated at the center of the solar system (heliocentrism, *helio* = sun), overturning the accepted and assumed cosmology of over a millennium and a half presented by Claudius Ptolemaeus. Luther's and Calvin's responses to these findings were unequivocal: Copernicus and Galileo were considered heretics for not submitting their science to the Word of God and therefore were worthy of being burned at the stake.

Hindsight gives us the huge advantage of seeing the conflict clearly. Luther and Calvin didn't realize how much of their Christianity and biblical understanding were meshed with the current culture of the day. In this particular case, they were reading the Bible through the lens of prevailing cosmology and assuming that this description could never change. In contemporary biblical studies we have since adopted principles of Bible study that *accommodate* the worldview of the biblical characters. We realize that they couldn't have had any other worldview than the one they were exposed to, and therefore we have to accommodate their historical milieu when we read the text.

All Christianity is expressed through culture. There is no neutral and correct version, only cultural expressions attempting to faithfully reflect the biblical witness. For me, the best way to summarize the problem Luther and Calvin faced is this: They simply didn't know how to disembed their understanding of Christianity from a departing medieval worldview and how to engage a newly emerging modern worldview. This sort of disembedding and reembedding process will always require new renderings of old ideas. Many of these ideas are sacred cows that have become confused with the unchanging and abiding truth.

I'm afraid that if we're not careful, we will do a rerun of *The Luther/Calvin Show*. Luther and Calvin got a lot of things right, but on this issue of quoting chapter and verse to prove geocentrism, they were dead wrong. Of course their motives were right. Of course they were simply trying to maintain a high and faithful view of Scripture. But we still have to ask this question: Will we learn from them, or will we bury our heads in the sand? We need a fuller, unabridged biblical story and an approach to spiritual conversations that are in sync with the architecture of the human heart. Learning these things will not be easy and will require deep shifts in our fundamental understanding of truth.

If you are up for profound transformation, and if you want to get serious about the full-calorie version of God's story and its implications for spiritual conversations, you are in for a journey. We are about to change the starting point of the conversation—and such a change will propel us into bigger and life-defining narratives.

Architecture

The metaphor of *architecture* emerges from a couple of different associations. Architecture can be about *building and design*—the elements necessary to create a final project. To those of you who have this sort of artistic, creative design disposition, you will hear the metaphor this way. But architecture can also be seen through the lens of *software and computer design*. When a software program is designed for a computer, there are several layers of communication within the program required for it to work. The software has to communicate with an operating system, such as Windows Vista or Mac OS X Leopard. The software also has to interact with the graphical user interface (GUI). These layers of communication have to be built into the software's design. This structure is referred to as the software's *architecture*. In many ways, the idea is similar to brick-and-mortar physical architecture, but if you are more familiar with computerese, then this metaphor may be the one that comes to your mind more frequently.

Whatever metaphor you find yourself accessing, the thought behind the title is the same: We have been specifically built—architected—with core design elements that cause us to crave transformation. Our ability to listen for the expression of these design elements in people's lives will always give us the most grist for spiritual conversations. These core design elements are constantly being expressed. If we can develop listening ears for our friends' hints and clues, we will find ourselves thick in all sorts of God-talk.

Part 1

The Three Texts

Spiritual conversations and our spiritual lives don't exist in a vacuum. The interplay of three components creates the environment where these occur. The *context* is obviously crucial. Context is everything from geography to culture. This text is important to understand because it provides the "container" in which everything in life transpires.

The *biblical* text contains the sweeping narrative of God's work and intention for the cosmos. The overarching story of God is what we claim to herald. Our understanding of this is absolutely critical if we are to make clear what God invites the world to experience.

The *human* text, our human story, is not only the broad story of the human condition but the unique stories of our particular geographical region, say the United States, as well as our own highly individualized stories. These three — the human story, the stories within our ethnicities and geographies, and our own personal life histories — are important shapers of how spiritual conversations can and do evolve.

All three of these texts require our attention and probing. We have to understand the *biblical text* and how it must be translated over and over again into the target *context*. How the biblical message translates into the tribal context of Burundi or Senegal is very different from how it translates into the corporate business world of Manhattan. The kind of translation talked about here isn't language; it is cultural and contextual. Furthermore, we have to understand that, while the human condition has fundamental similarities across cultural spectrums, the way the human condition takes on unique hues and tones in various contexts means we have to be sensitive.

The chapters in this section help us think about these three texts in the hope that we will do a better job of understanding all three so we can move comfortably among them and gain awareness of how they interface.

The Context

Whenever I saw Chad, a superficial thought would come to mind: "I sure wish I had his ripped arms!" Growing up, I had always been the skinny kid, and it hasn't changed much. I still can't do more than four chin-ups. Chad and I met while working out on elliptical machines in our health club. He is one of those guys who is in amazing shape for his age. He is several years my senior, but his workout or eating regimen seems to be keeping the ticking age clock at bay. We had seen each other in the club for months but had never had a serious interaction until what I did for a living came up in conversation.

"You used to be a pastor?" he blurted out. "You're kidding, right?"

"Really and truly I was," I said with the why-is-that-so-surprising look I always shoot at people when they are shocked at my background—though I have to admit I do not fit the stereotype of a pastor. "And now I'm a church consultant, which means I'm a long-distance staffer for several churches."

"Well, then, we need to talk. I have all sorts of questions, and none of them have quick answers. I'm pretty interested in spiritual things, even in guys like Gandhi and Jesus; but the institutions set up by followers of these guys don't impress me much." Our spiritual conversations began that day and continued over the next year and a half.

Not long after that initial encounter, Chad and I began to meet each other on the golf course, enjoying daylight saving time and the reality of twilight golf. The golf course is such a great place to see beauty and just be quiet and settle a hurried and harried mind—but this only happens for me if my game is playing out as beautifully as the surroundings. And this particular night had been no such time. And now we stood in the parking lot in semidarkness.

As Chad shoved his clubs into the truck, he said, "Hey, Ron, what do you know about the axial age?"

I still had my clubs hanging from my shoulder, but with a question like that, there was no reason to be a golf club rack. So I flipped off the strap and set up the bag on its pop-out stand and began rummaging in my pockets to pull out all my tees, ball markers, and divot repair tools. As I continued my pocket mining, I looked up. "I am no expert, but I do know a tiny bit about it because it was such a fertile era for global religious development. I can tell you just about all I know in a couple sentences."

"Go ahead."

"The axial age was the time period between 800–200 BC when some key religious figures and movements were born in China, India, the Middle East, and certain places in the West—movements that still nourish many of the spiritual traditions of our day. I can't remember for sure, but I think the term was first used by the famous philosopher-historian Karl Jaspers."

Chad nodded, and even in the dying light I could see he was interested in what I was saying.

"I could give you a few more details, but come on, Chad. This is a pretty obscure question. Am I supposed to ask if there is a Double Jeopardy follow-up question, Alex?"

Chad laughed and leaned against the bumper of the car as I pulled a club out of my bag to take a practice swing. "Well, Ron, I've been reading a book by Karen Armstrong, and she thinks we may be in another axial age of sorts."

While I hadn't read it, I was familiar with her 2006 book called *The Great Transformation*, in which she plays off Jaspers' well-known *The Origin and Goal of History* written in the mid-1950s.

The air had changed, and the humidity of the early evening could be felt as the golf course went into a quiet hibernation for the night. It was one of the course's most peaceful and beautiful times. "Armstrong has a sense that many of the major religions of today have to undergo something of a reconfiguration if we are to have any voice in today's context," Chad said. "What do you think?" But he didn't even give me time to jump in. "Personally, I think she's on to something. You know, I'm a fan of Moby and his music, and I was on his website the other night surfing around. You know what he says about Jesus?"

I simply gave Chad a raised eyebrow and a slight shrug. It was enough to give him the airspace to continue — which I was quite sure he was going to do, permission or not.

"Funny how these things sort of dovetail," he said. "I wrote it down because it is such a great example of how I feel and what I would like to talk to you about."

He reached into the trunk of his car, flipped open his red and black North Face backpack, and produced a tattered spiral notebook. He thumbed through the pages to get to the back and then handed me the notebook. "Take a look at this and see what you think."

The words from Moby were scrawled in blue ink:

> i actually think that the teachings of christ accomodate most of the new ways in which we perceive ourselves and our world.
>
> the problem is that although the teachings of christ accomodate this, contemporary christianity does not.
>
> here's more seriousness dressed up as flippancy:
>
> christ: acknowledging quantum realities.
>
> christianity: depressingly newtonian.
>
> does that make any sense?
>
> well, to me it does.
>
> and to some of you it might make sense, also.[1]

Moby is dead-on, I thought. Truth is, this is what a lot of people outside the church think; but not just that—it's what a lot of people inside the church think, people like me! I wasn't sure how forthright to be with Chad at this stage in our exploration. I was still trying to listen to him, not talk, assume, or insert too much. We had had a few conversations, but this was the first time it felt like we were digging into something substantial.

"Moby pretty much summarizes my view," Chad said. "We need a new faith and new church—a new something to align more with the founder's intent. My issue isn't Jesus; it is Jesus-ians. It isn't Christ that is the problem; it is Christians."

I was standing next to my bag, with my hand on my three-wood head cover, and I nodded to let Chad know I was totally tracking with him and agreeing with what he was saying.

"You know, Ron," Chad continued, "I grew up in the church,

left it in college, and just have no interest in the typical narrow understanding that seems so predictable in the church. I wouldn't consider myself any more a Christian than a Muslim or Buddhist. Are Christians all idiots who check their minds at the door?"

I winced at this comment. Chad saw my face.

"I admit I may be overstating things a bit," he continued. "But you know what? The incongruity between what is claimed and what is lived is just excruciating. I think I can go with there may be a God, but maybe not. I think there is something bigger than me, some overarching power, spirit, something—but I'm not one bit convinced it is the Judeo-Christian God."

"Chad, I really do agree with many of the things you are saying," I said. "I think we could have some great conversations learning from each other. How serious are you about wanting to really engage in this conversation?"

"How much time do you have?" Chad asked. "How about we make this twilight golf time a regular Tuesday connection time, and we can mix golf and talk? What do you think?"

I was all in—and hence started my serious spiritual conversations with Chad.

Change Is in the Air

Chad is an intelligent guy who has spiritual interest but is unsure of how to progress. He has areas of real hostility, issues of doubt, questions about whether or not the Christian rendition of God even exists. All of this is held simultaneously and comfortably with his belief that Jesus was a historical person and a pretty good guy.

My guess is that the world has lots of Chads. Lots of people I know are trying to figure out if Christianity can handle their toughest questions, their random musings, and their deepest doubts. As I talk to these friends and acquaintances, what emerges is the reality that times *have* changed. The cultural container in which we live has undergone a seismic change, and what was once off-limits is now mainstream conversation.

Like countless others, Chad is a guy who wants to talk about the journey, be on the journey, explore paths and trails of the journey, but he doesn't want to let anyone short-circuit the journey or tell him exactly which steps and direction the journey should take. Chad is responding to the way he has been designed on the inside. Something about what he senses deep inside leads him to think that this journey is worth pursuing.

Chad is representative of a much larger group of people in the United States who are on a spiritual quest and looking for conversation partners but are uninterested in pat, canned, certain, scripted, prepackaged answers.

Before we can really engage the topic of spiritual conversation, we need to consider the context in which the conversation is happening. We need to understand the present shift so we can enter those arenas informed and articulate. We have a word we use for the "context we are in" — *culture*. We need to take a quick cultural tour.

The label *culture* was formulated in the late eighteenth century and comes from the Latin word *cultus*, which literally means "care" or "careful treatment."[2] Culture in our world has come to mean the unwritten and often unspoken ways we are to conduct ourselves in relation to each other, as well as the artifacts and structures we create and use to make these interactions work.

Why is this so important? Chad has already brought up authors, musicians, and ideas that are part of the cultural currency. These ideas and figures are part of the cultural container in which he is living, moving, and breathing. If we want to intelligently interact with people today, if we want to understand what makes them tick, then we need to understand these phenomena.

And it is not just trends and fads I am talking about here. While those are important and helpful for understanding a snapshot in time, fads tend to come and go quickly. The seismic changes going on right now are historically, culturally, and scientifically dramatic. These are epochal shifts, and these changes have to do with the transition to a new era. The important thing for our conversation is the fact that the tectonic plates shifting under the surface are provoking interest in a variety of spiritual things.

What is going on in our culture that has enabled a guy like Chad to want to have conversations about such things as the axial age? Other than university students studying history, who is going around talking about the axial age? This is simply one indicator of the kind of information (another sign of the time) available to the masses. This sort of knowledge not long ago would have been thought arcane and obscure. Not anymore. It is now available in national best sellers and local coffee shop conversations.

A quick comparison of national best-selling books, TV talk show topics, and research polls from fifteen years ago and from today will yield plenty of evidence for an increased spiritual interest. Deepak Chopra, Eckhart Tolle, Oprah Winfrey, Wayne Dyer, and a plethora of other New Age resources only scratch the surface of the conversation going on around us.

And this spiritual interest seems to be growing *outside* the church. The statistics of mass exodus from the church—and not by the disgruntled and disenfranchised but by the most dynamic and faith-filled followers—demonstrate that spiritual investigation is happening primarily outside the walls of the church. For some, this may feel like a fresh spring breeze. For all of us, this means we must take the questions seriously.

The modern world with all of its promises of technological advance hasn't brought with it a proportional amount of relief, a better global life, or a deeper sense of purpose for the world. One of the main tenets of the modern world—the promise of a better tomorrow through technology—has been dashed by two world wars, genocide, dictatorial regimes that continue, HIV/ AIDS, September 11, a continuing war-torn Middle East, human slavery, and an ecological system so far out of whack we wonder at times how many more tomorrows we have left.

While we won't take an in-depth look at all of these, we do need to recognize and note how these issues have created shifts in our culture that feed directly into the spiritual hunger of people in the West. Examining a few of these shifts not only will help us get our bearings in the crazy world we live in but, as importantly, will give us a better lay of the spiritual land of the people we interact with every day—the ones who aren't finding their way to churches for their spiritual explorations.

The Shift from Newton to Quantum — The Relational Value

The modern world's view that reality is whatever can be touched, tasted, measured, quantified, observed, and categorized is the heritage of the Enlightenment. That world of microscopes and telescopes, of beakers and Bunsen burners, of facts and figures, is slowly losing its footing. We are living in an era where the predictability of an "A causes B" world is slowly fading from the scene. This is true of life on both a practical level and a scientific and philosophical level.

One of my family members, who was well established in the upper levels of management in a large company, was called into the office and let go because "we think this is better for us and you." He had absolutely no warning, no explanation, no reward for years of committed work—not even a hint from the boss, with whom he had spent each day in a close working relationship. This could happen to anyone at any time, of course; but it wasn't common twenty years ago. The stock-and-trade expectation of our parents' generation (or their parents' generation) was that you give blood for the company for thirty to thirty-five years, take retirement, and live off the well-earned pension built through long-term staying power. That experience is a distant relic of yesteryear.

While this is only one recent example of the creeping unpredictability in our lives, it is an illustration of the shift we have undergone from our Newtonian cause-and-effect worldview to the highly relational, interconnected, and what at times appears to be a random but well-webbed quantum world. If A caused B in the old world, in the new world B seems to be caused more by an invisible C or D or X or Y.

Our observations and even experiences of deep relational interconnectedness are what our quantum world and systems theory are all about. These two arenas of exploration are the reason for abandoning the largely mechanical worldview of cause-and-effect linear modernity.

In the modern era, life and world were seen as a machine. Our metaphors even reflected this unwitting adoption of the machine-like worldview we grew to love. We talked of hitting on all eight cylinders, keeping the machine well-oiled, planting your feet on solid ground, grounding your conclusions in hard research, needing crystal clarity about opinions and data, being a solid rock in hard times. Do you see what all these have in common? Stability, firmness, machinelike consistency, hardness, solidity. Our lives, we thought, were encased in the world of machine, and our metaphors reflected just that certainty.

So where do spiritual things fit in the modern world of machine? Not surprisingly, "second-class citizen" or "supplemental" is the classification they often receive.[3]

Note not only the hard metaphors and phrases we have mentioned but how the opposites have been viewed in the same machine world. The words *soft* or *squishy* are usually considered derogatory. When lines are too fluid or blurry, that is a bad thing. When people change their mind, they have gone soft or become wishy-washy. Rock hard and crystal clear are preferable to soft and watered-down in the mechanical world of modernity.

In the last several decades interesting things have happened that have changed the whole playing field of the predictable machine-like world of modernity. Those changes have massive implications for spiritual conversations and for the transformational longings that people seem to be freer than ever to talk about and pursue.

Science and hard data formed the machinelike modern world and relegated spiritual things to the conversation margins. This was the modern world container or context in which spiritual conversations happened—or, more often than not, didn't happen. But a revolution has been underway. Science has been in the process of uncovering a highly relational, even spiritual foundation for our world—and like all relationships, we are being reacquainted with unpredictability and uncertainty. At the level of science, this relationality is referred to as "the quantum world." It is the shift from seeing the world as machine to seeing the world as a living, breathing organism. When you see the world as alive instead of as a machine, how we view life, how we speak about the world, how we interpret reality — it all changes.

If the first big revolution of mind was the Enlightenment and the rise of rationalism and the birth of the modern world, we are living in what might be called the second great revolution of mind and spirit. Social scientist Willis Harman has argued that we may be living in what will prove to be the most significant shift of all time. Harman says we are entering a second Copernican revolution. He writes, "Whereas the original Copernican revolution reordered our concepts of outer space, this one is concerned with our understanding of inner space."[4] This, perhaps more than anything else in our culture, is sowing seeds of spiritual interest that are quietly growing but dramatically and powerfully shaping the cultural conversation.

Harman goes on to explain how this second Copernican revolution is a shift from an M1 to an M3 worldview. In the M1 world, the basic stuff of the universe is *matter*. Whatever consciousness or soul that exists emerges out of matter. In other words, there is no such thing as God or God's Spirit; anything that looks like "God" is simply highly evolved matter. According to this worldview, we aren't spiritual beings; we are simply highly evolved material beings. This has been the prevailing and dominant worldview of the twentieth century and has informed the scientific method. Whatever you can taste, touch, hear, see, and smell is reality; if the five senses can't get at it, it doesn't exist. The modern world, devoid of God, relegated religion to a mere vapor trail where it had once been a significant shaping force on the cultural landscape. This is the essence of what is often referred to as secularism — looking at the world apart from any language or perspective of the gods.

In the M2 world, there are two fundamentally different types of material—*matter-energy stuff* and *mind-spirit stuff*. This is what is typically called dualism for the obvious reason that it points to two different things. Interestingly, this view is what many Christians hold, even though it isn't the view found in Scripture. Many Christians think there are two different realms that are largely unconnected—the world of matter and the world of spirit—and the two never meet except in the incarnation of Jesus.

In the M3 world, the ultimate stuff of the universe is *mind-spirit*. Out of the mind-spirit stuff comes the material world. Therefore, the only way to contact the deepest stuff of the universe is through mind-spirit avenues. A quick glance at the book of Genesis reveals that this is really what the traditional Christian world and life view has held. God is primary and before all matter, and when God spoke, he as Spirit brought forth matter into existence.

So much for the metaphysics lesson. What's the point, the punch line? Willis Harman says that for several hundred years we have lived almost exclusively with an M1 worldview. Any conversation about the world of the spirit or the world of an invisible God was simply relegated to a mythic, less advanced, more primitive worldview. But here is the catch: Harman's whole argument is that we are living in the time period when we are experiencing a shift from a predominantly M1 world to a predominantly M3 world.

It's hard to imagine what this means for spiritual conversation in our culture. What was just a decade ago somewhat embarrassing to have conversations about—the world of the spirit—is now not only acceptable, but we even have TV shows and movies in which these are presumed worldview components. Oprah Winfrey speaks about it regularly. One of her latest endeavors is the ten-week live webcast with Eckhart Tolle on the content of his latest book, *A New Earth: Awakening to Your Life's Purpose.* How many people are now engaging this worldview because of her?

In this new M3 world, the interconnection of all things, the deeply relational web, is primary. The world is alive; it is not a machine. Everything in the world is connected to everything else in the world. This is the finding of quantum mechanics, which along with other discoveries is turning our understanding of the world upside down or, maybe more aptly, inside out.

Take, for instance, the now famous Bell's theorem from the 1960s, which physicist Henry Stapp called "the most profound discovery of science."[5] Essentially Bell's theorem and experiments in nonlocal causality demonstrated that paired electrons that are split apart and separated by thousands of miles are totally connected in some invisible way. When one electron's spin was changed, the other electron thousands of miles away would instantaneously reverse its spin.

And the big deal is?

Well, what this experiment—replicated numerous times— shows is that our world at the atomic level is connected by something invisible. In some quiet, invisible yet apparently tangible way we are all related at some level. In short, the world is deeply relational, deeply connected. This conclusion is in keeping with the shift to an M3 view of the world. Quantum physicist David Bohm calls it the "implicate order," the deeply connected relational nature of all reality.[6]

The implications for spiritual conversations are significant. As these discoveries are being made—many of them in our lifetime—it opens public discourse to spiritual conversation. The discoveries seem to point to some deeper connective reality, something we have always held to and believed. Essentially, the world is coming around to embrace an M3 world in which conversations about the connective tissue of all things can be discussed.

Our culture is coming to understand our world as a very different place from what we thought it was less than a generation ago.[7] These new learnings—learnings trumpeted on the covers of all major periodicals—are giving people permission to see spiritual things as core components of our very existence. I am not suggesting that we should take our cues from discoveries science does or doesn't make. What I am suggesting is that the current conversations in science have made spiritual conversations more legitimate and widespread and are bringing us closer than we have been in several hundred years to seeing the interconnection of things material and spiritual. For us to be informed about these issues only makes sense; they are great grist for our conversations as Christ-followers.

In the midst of these discoveries we see a rather virulent backlash coming from some of the atheistic minds of our times. Authors such as Richard Dawkins and Sam Harris continue their publishing unabated, as they vie and evangelize for the M1 world. Only time will tell how many people they can "convert" with their writing and debating.

Jacques Derrida, one of the seminal French philosophers in deconstructionism and postmodernism, says that the technologies we have used in our advances in science are the very tools that have brought a revival of interest in the divine.[8] Technology, once the certainty bringer, is moving us into space Derrida calls "animistic, magical, and mystical."[9] Science has let a sense of mystery and unknown back in, and that can be nothing but a good thing for the conversation.

The reentry of mystery is in part the result of a more chastened certainty, which helps us understand that our perspective—what we bring to any observation—guides and shapes what we see, making our understandings of life far more person-specific than we had originally thought. Objectivity just isn't a possibility in the sort of "hard-core science" definition of things. All viewing of life is through my lens, and my lens is, as the apostle Paul says, dim and dark (see 1 Corinthians 13:12). The shift from Newton to quantum is indeed one of the big denominators in the rise of spiritual conversation possibilities in our culture.

The Shift from Naïveté to 9/11 — The Reality Check Value

In the modern world of the West, technology, military strength, an empire mentality, affluence, and an unquenchable sense of self, coupled with an insatiable appetite of entitlement, had created a naïveté that nothing could possibly slow us down, let alone stop us in our tracks. This modern American myth of invincibility and progress was at the heart of cultural self-understanding for at least the last half of the twentieth century. But everything was about to change.

I was sitting in my office doing a consultation with eight staff members from a church on issues they were struggling with, when my administrative assistant stuck her head in my office and said that a plane had just crashed into one of the Twin Towers in New York City. We all remember where we were as the events of that day unfolded, and we realized it wasn't an accident when another plane hit the second tower. Our myth of invincibility was crumbling as quickly and forcefully as the steel girders and concrete of those two iconic towers. The indelible memory mark left on those alive when it happened may be incomparable to anything Americans witnessed in the same lifetime.

The power of the 9/11 event was as much myth shaking as it was life shattering. The United States—standing tall in a post–Cold War, Manifest Destiny ethos—experienced the crumbling both figuratively and literally of our economic supremacy and the visual symbols of our strength and dominance. With years behind us, we now know it was a watershed event, a redefining moment in our personal and historical consciousness.

In the wake of 9/11, religious traditions that had barely ever talked to each other hosted joint interfaith prayer meetings. Some attempted to interpret the events of 9/11 in light of God's judgment; others were quick to point to the Devil as the one clearly behind such fundamentalist lunacy. Some cried out to God for comfort; others raged at God—but that our naïveté was now a thing of the past was something everyone could agree on.

Cultural conditions always set the container for conversation. In our post-9/11 world it is no different. The idea that I am safe, invulnerable, sequestered, and protected inside the neat and tidy borders of Kingdom America is now a belief of the past. For if in a split second an entire nation can be brought to its knees, then surely my life is not inviolable. And yet in the bleak days and months following the tragedy, despair and grief were slowly replaced by hope. I will return often to the theme of hope in this book because it appears to be one of the hardwired design elements found within every human heart, no matter where or when they have lived.

In a world where I am vulnerable, in a world of violence where senseless and random killings are nightly news, in a world where tsunamis, earthquakes, and wildfires happen with a capriciousness that should lead to despair, we experienced the phenomenon of *The Purpose Driven Life*, a book read by nearly thirty million people to help them find their purpose in life.[10] Our post-9/11-

punctured naïveté tenderizes the human spirit. While in some cases it may breed bitterness against God, in many cases the "why" question allows powerful entry points to ongoing conversation. The "how is God at work in these tough circumstances" question is what might be referred to as the *visio* component of faith development. *Visio*, the Latin root word from which we get the word *vision*, is how we see God at work in the affairs of everyday life. How do we see God interacting? Is it positive, neutral, or negative? Terrorism, natural disasters, and epidemics such as HIV/AIDS all raise *visio* questions—those questions that by definition are spiritual.

The Shift from Proposition to Praxis —
The Action Value

If the shift from a Newtonian world to a quantum world helps us get in touch with the deeply relational nature of all things, and if our naïveté has now been chastened by destructive and inexplicable events so that we are asking God-related questions, then what of our taste for all sorts of talk and little action? One of the conditions in our culture, largely a product of the modern world, is our love affair with text and hypertext, our interest in information, our penchant for extracting propositions. The Internet is only the latest avenue for proliferating information, but before that there was TV, radio, books, and print media. And we continue to escalate and accelerate the flow of information.

In many ways, this is a good thing. We live in a place on the historical timeline where for the first time, patients can bring in information for their doctors, and students can actually verify what their teachers say. Having three teenagers, I know firsthand that high school teachers have on occasion been corrected by student knowledge garnered from the Internet. Information proliferates, and with this proliferation comes the illusion of progress. You can learn a lot online about anything you can think of—but there is no assurance that the information you receive will in any way change your life.

The "information 'in' = life change 'out'" equation has been a problematic one since the beginning of time. The illusion that when you take in information, your life must somehow be undergoing a transformation is as old as the hills. But this equation has been found desperately inaccurate in church circles for years. We have equated church attendance, Bible study attendance, small group attendance, Sunday school attendance, Bible reading consistency, and other input-type channels as the litmus tests of growing Christians.[11] The same sort of equation can be identified in our educational systems as well. Short-term memory cramming regurgitated on an exam will usually get a high mark. No real application is necessary or even important.

Attendance at all the church functions in no way ensures any life change. In fact, some might be tempted to argue that the more information you take in, the more you may be lulled into thinking the information flow is the point instead of the life transformation it is supposed to evoke. Most church folks know plenty of people who have sat through years of great sermons and Bible studies and are no more patient today than last year or last decade, are no more loving to those difficult people around them, are no more broken for the plight of the world, and really look no more like Jesus than they did at the beginning of the journey. In fact, when we dare to be brutally honest, many of us see in our own lives the same stalled spiritual formation and flirtation with information we can so readily identify in others.

The Bible has warned us about this. James said to be doers, not just hearers (see James 1:22–25). But the acuteness of such a warning seems more poignant today than ever. You can hear with regularity the criticism from without and within—that the church is full of hypocrites, full of those who don't practice what they preach and don't walk their talk. The short translation of those phrases? *We don't act on what we hear.*

The need for authenticity and living out faith are such crying needs, even at the theological level where information is paramount, that Kevin Vanhoozer has written a massive volume titled *The Drama of Doctrine*, in which he argues for a dramatic theater-type play setting where actual doctrine is lived out in the narrative play of life. We are actors in the performance of a *"theo-drama,"* he says. He even goes as far as to talk about our need for a post-propositional atonement—an understanding of atonement that is more than simply a list of principles.[12]

The outcry against and reaction to propositional overload is leading many people to say, "Show me. Live it. Demonstrate it. Get dirty and do it." We are living in the era of *Extreme Makeover, Three Wishes, Your Life or Your Money,* and a whole bevy of other shows that illustrate and elevate the action-oriented, "git 'er done" value, the "quit talking and just do it" value. When you look at what qualifies for leadership and membership in a church, it is almost exclusively built around propositional belief systems. If you believe what we believe—and sometimes behave how we behave—then you can belong. Unfortunately, ongoing life change rarely is the litmus test of leadership enlistment or church membership. As we read the Gospels, however, Jesus seemed very, very short on doctrine and very, very big on life change.

People seem to be crying out for action. Action that demonstrates life change, action that embraces risk in standing for values that run counter to imperialism and consumerism, action that shows information being translated into softer, bigger, more compassionate hearts. Our culture is tired of empty propositions and parroted platitudes. People are looking for embodiment; a full-blown living *into* the life of difference making.

Hooray for the church whose people want to do more than huddle around Sunday morning campfires, sing "Kumbaya," and receive yet another brain dump from a pastor who has hunkered in the bastion of his office for twenty hours to prepare his thirty-minute masterpiece. There is certainly a biblical model in which Jesus emerges from a context of solitude and goes to the synagogue to speak or to the crowds to teach. The emphasis on knowledge acquisition as the primary scorecard of life change, however, seems more a product of the modern post-Enlightenment world—the world of lecture, information flow, and textual elevation. Jesus seemed to model a balance between knowledge and practice.

Consider the sanctuary/auditorium design in our churches for the last several hundred years. People sit out there and listen to someone who climbs behind a lectern to lecture. The very design of our church buildings betrays this rationalist elevation. From what should we take our cues—post-Enlightenment rationalism or something closer to the relational dynamic Jesus modeled and the early church seemed to imbibe?

I see this desire for a consistency in our talk *and* action as a good sign. For some churches, it is finally their day to show the world how the shalom of God, his gift of peace, wholeness, well-being, is translated into real action and world-changing *inter*action. In fact, I think this action bias may prove to be one of the most important conversation starters about spiritual things we could envision. For other churches, this fed-up attitude will be their death knell, the final beeping on the life support systems they have been on for a while. It is only a matter of time before they slowly shut down and die.

To be aware of this cultural phenomenon—and to stop talking and start taking action to help the world—is to become aware of a major entry point into the conversation. *Time* magazine put a rock star along with one of the smartest and wealthiest computer wizards and his wife on its cover because Bono and Bill and Melinda Gates are attempting to put their money where their mouths are—and not just their money but also their time and energy—to change the world.[13] That should tell us something about what people are craving. Those around us see the brokenness of the world, and they want to do something about it.

The Shift from Brokenness to Wholeness — The Shalom Value

Brokenness is a huge reality on the cultural radar and a dominant entry point for spiritual conversation because technology has made pain "glocal"—a global phenomenon felt at the local level. While many people do not make the connection between brokenness and the need for God, the link often lurks in the quiet recesses of many people's minds. Unfortunately, Christians have often modeled God's love so poorly that people just don't see God as a significant part of the solution.

From disaster relief in places like Thailand and New Orleans to ongoing war in various countries in the Middle East, to genocide, to child slavery and child soldiers, to atrocities in Darfur, to massive problems of hunger, safe drinking water, and illiteracy in our own backyard—brokenness abounds. These public issues have given rise to the Copenhagen Consensus Center, the UN

Millennium Development Goals initiative, and many other social impact programs.[14]

It takes significant grist to understand the cultural context into which we have been called to have conversation. At the Copenhagen Consensus 2006 meeting in New York, the countries represented were Angola, Australia, Belarus, Canada, China, Denmark, Germany, India, Iraq, Mexico, Niger, Pakistan, Poland, Republic of Korea, Slovenia, Somalia, Tanzania, Thailand, Uganda, United Arab Emirates, the United States, Vietnam, Zambia, and Zimbabwe. In 2004, a group of international economists and think tank experts convened to define and detail the biggest problems the world faces. The result? A list of the ten greatest global challenges: climate change, communicable diseases, conflicts and arms proliferation, education, financial instability, governance and corruption, malnutrition and hunger, migration, sanitation and clean water, and subsidies and trade barriers. The conversation ended with reflections on a hypothetical question: If the global village had $50 billion—billion, with a *b*—to solve the biggest issues the world faces, how should we spend that money? To see the results, go their website.[15] My point is, these sorts of initiatives and conversations bring the issue of God's role in the world forum to the forefront of discussion. These are interesting and valuable spiritual conversation starting points for those who have a sense of global consciousness.

While some of these committees and reports are confined to the world of the specialist, certainly the "wristband phenomenon" is a grassroots groundswell. From Bono's ONE campaign to Lance Armstrong's LIVE**STRONG** yellow wristbands, which have sold nearly fifty million units to date, a large number of people have parted with a dollar to join a cause. And this is only the beginning. The (Product)[RED] initiatives for the support of the Global Fund to Fight AIDS, Tuberculosis and Malaria—and a host of similar ideas around fair trade and helping others in the world—only serve to reinforce that a global consciousness is taking hold in our world.

The idea that our world is in trouble on a number of fronts and that we need to recognize our deep connectedness as a global people is the subject of David Korten's latest book *The Great Turning*. The subtitle summarizes the necessary shift: *From Empire to Earth Community.*[16] His global insights are jarring, as is his interpretation of Christian history. These observations serve as the context for the unfolding human stories of the people with whom we live and work. For us to be ignorant or even inattentive to the themes of the day is to miss a major shaper of the American conversation. I think most people are longing for a world where shalom exists, where people practice it, and where its results overwhelm the emptiness and brokenness so prevalent in the world today. This is the landscape in which we live.

If the landscape is giving rise to spiritual conversations, what has been the outcome in the spiritual arena? That people are seeking spiritual experience is so obvious as to be ridiculous to cite. In the time of the greatest advancements on the planet, the shrinking of the world into a global community through technology and communication—during the time of the greatest affluence ever seen (in the West, that is)—what is driving this spiritual quest?

Perhaps the parenthetical phrase "in the West" may have something to do with it, as do the shifts mentioned above.

For all the apparent advances, we feel empty. For all the shrinking of the globe, we feel the pain of the people in the rest of the world in different ways, even though we have never met them. For all of our Western affluence, we feel a deep-down, gnawing guilt that somehow the inequities of the world really are a tragedy. All of that, and probably a host of other subtler and more complex factors, puts us on a quest for something spiritual—something to make sense of it all—and for a way to be a vehicle of wholeness and completeness in the midst of a shattered and broken cosmos. This quest has had an interesting path.

The Quest for Spiritual Wholeness

In our typical consumeristic Western way, our self-made and designed spirituality seemed to be the buzz of the late 1990s and into the turn of the millennium. Our ability—through creams, gels, and surgeries, not to mention every imaginable gadget—to sculpt and design our bodies in an attempt to control the effects of the toll of time seems to be the impetus for something similar in the realm of the spiritual. Self-help endeavors and the search for spiritual experiences in everything from yoga to meditation classes to philosophical enquiries to a renewed exploration of tantric sexuality—all of these and more have become the questing venues of a culture empty but hoping.

More than ever, a mixture of Christian, Hindu, Buddhist, New Age, and Wiccan beliefs have been stirred into a spiritual stew to satisfy any appetite. Apparently, however, this spate of interest has not located the magic elixir, the fountain of youth, the spiritual amalgam, to satiate our spiritual craving. The intensity of the quest for things spiritual seems to move at an unabated clip. What can we as Christ-followers hope to say to this? What possible role can we play in the conversation? Do we have anything whatsoever to contribute?

The church should be the place people go to seek connection to God, to explore spirituality, to deeply experience and engage shalom—peace, wholeness, wellness. But that too, at least for the moment, is a thing of the past. Researcher George Barna contends

that we are currently experiencing the most significant movement of Christians in the last 100 years—a movement of those
in the church who are slowly migrating outside of the confines
of the church. And their migration isn't because they are newly
converted God-haters or have lost faith amid the onslaught of
the writings of Richard Dawkins and Sam Harris and others like
them. They are leaving because their faith isn't being nurtured.
They are simply not experiencing God. Consider these statistics:

- Eight out of ten believers don't feel they experience a
  connection with God or feel God's presence in a worship
  service.

- Half of all believers do not feel they have entered the
  presence of God or experienced a genuine connection with
  God during the past year.

- The typical churched believer will die without ever leading
  one person to become a follower of Jesus.[17]

Quite clearly the local church is not the hope of the world, contrary to what many pastors parrot. The only hope is Jesus.

All of these factors taken together form an interesting web.
Where are people to look for what they are seeking? Maybe an
even more basic question is, "For what are they seeking; for what
are they *yearning*?" If we can come to better understand what
people are yearning for, do we have any clues that may help seeds
germinate?

An Axial Shift

It may be helpful to review one more macro condition. In my
chapter 1 conversation with Chad, I mentioned the 1953 book by

Karl Jaspers titled *The Origin and Goal of History* in which he identified what he called "the axial age"—the era between 800 and
200 BC. Jaspers identified a number of characteristics that marked
this age as unique, but one of the most important was the birth
and rise of several key religious figures and movements in different
parts of the world—including Socrates and Plato and other Greek
rationalist philosophers such as Parmenides, Heraclitus, Homer,
Thucydides, and Archimedes, who would later nourish much of
the Western world and have a profound influence on Christianity. In India, Hinduism and Jainism developed, and this era saw
the birth of Siddhartha Gautama, the founder of Buddhism. In
Persia, Zoroaster came onto the scene. In China, Confucianism
was born, and it still has significant impact on ethics and life in
large regions of Asia. During this same time period in the Middle
East the writings of Judaism's major prophets—Isaiah, Jeremiah,
Ezekiel—emerged.

You may ask what this has to do with spiritual conversations
and why Chad would be interested. As you recall, Chad had told
me about reading Karen Armstrong's book *The Great Transformation*, which argued that a new axial age of sorts is dawning—an
age where a significant reconfiguration of the world's great religious traditions must happen if they are to have any bearing and
relevance for the people of our world.[18]

In a recent interview with *What Is Enlightenment?* magazine,
Armstrong notes that the first axial age occurred when individualism was just dawning.[19] Urbanization was taking hold and
people were living in increasingly commercial, market-driven
economies. The rise of new economic realities was bringing to
the forefront issues of equity—and with it came questions about
how to balance, monitor, and assure equity as groups of haves and
have-nots. Armstrong further observes that the emergence of *every*

spirituality was the result of a rejection of violence and a desire to look for sources of violence within the psyche of humanity. The great sages emerged in a world of great violence, horror, and societal suffering. In her opinion, this is the stage on which the great religions of the world became actors in the effort to help humanity find a deeper sense of meaning, comfort, and being. Armstrong suggests that now, in the first decade of the twenty-first century, we are living in a new axial age characterized by globalization.

Her connection of the axial age with a recognition of a new one occurring today is instructive. To say we are living in the beginning stages of a second axial age is both exhilarating and sobering. The need for Christianity to revoice the message has never been more important. Making sure we understand the message we are voicing should be a primary consideration.

This is another one of those interesting developments about our moment in history that neatly coincides with the shift from an M1 to an M3 worldview and the other currents I've mentioned—all giving rise to a unique and helpful context to consider as we pursue spiritual conversations.

Chad is only one of the many tuned into these currents. In some way he sees Karen Armstrong's evaluation as an indictment of the church, which has been unable to keep pace with the changes that need to be made to allow Christianity anything other than a mere peep from the margins of the dark halls of libraries.

With all of these cultural conditions and shifts, with these observations by students of philosophy and religious traditions, maybe we are ready to reexplore the story—God's big story. As I observed in my book *Static*, we need to retell God's big story—and do so in a way that connects to people who are living within the shifts we have just explored.

We are constantly navigating and learning about three texts—the context, the biblical text, and the human text. But with that, we'll also need to reenvision and recast the biblical text, as well as understand the human text—the architecture of the human condition—so we can see God's story in the human story. In that convergence we will find resonance with the deepest human longings.

CHAPTER 2

The Biblical Text

"Oh, Ron, this is so incredible! I simply can't believe what I'm learning at this stage in my life. Here I've grown up in the church, and *all* I've ever heard was, 'Jesus came and died for your sins—now go tell others about this.'"

Betty Sue is a sixty-four-year-old widow who is very hip and a smart businesswoman. And while she could retire, she has no intention to—being the "people person" she is. I had met her at one of the churches where I was doing "The Big Story" classes. She had been coming to the monthly Tuesday night class for over a year for the retelling of the unabbreviated, unabridged story of God.

"So tell me, what is clicking now, and when did all this start to happen?" I asked.

"Ron, I guess I am just blown away that so much of what I know is—well—not wrong, just horribly incomplete. The most exciting thing for me is here I am, a real estate agent. I talk with people every day who are dreaming about their life story. I know that sounds somewhat dramatic, but it's the truth. When people are buying homes, they're thinking about what it means to their families, the memories they'll make, the birthdays and anniversaries that will be celebrated there. People see their house purchase as part of their unfolding story, and until this year I would have never ever seen it or been able to articulate it."

"You are making all those connections yourself?"

She was blurting out a stream of consciousness, as though a plug had been inserted in a power source and her mental computer had suddenly come on.

"Well, Ron, all of a sudden—and I guess this isn't totally sudden, since we've been studying this for nearly a year—but all of a sudden in the last couple months the implications of this fuller story has really become clear. I have begun to translate what we are learning into my real estate business, and I realize this is actually ultrapractical. I think when we began talking about all this, I was skeptical. I've been in the Christian church my whole life. I have attended Bible studies and small groups for decades. So for you to start the story in a new place, for us to explore with a wide-angle lens, so to speak, well—initially, you know, I thought that was threatening. Remember all those questions and pushing around I did in class just eight or nine months ago?"

We both laughed and nodded our heads as if to say, "Who could forget all that verbal sparring?"

"I think the 'all of a sudden' feeling for me is I see so clearly how what originally was a Bible class has become the foundation for understanding how to enter spiritual conversations in a totally natural way in my business. And that's just pretty darn exciting!"

The CliffsNotes Version

Most Christians—at least those from predominantly evangelical backgrounds—know an abbreviated CliffsNotes version of the biblical story. It's important that we realize this, because it is precisely a miscue at the story level that causes a nearly complete failure at the spiritual conversation level.

Many of us have been guilty of telling an abbreviated and incomplete story of God's purposes on this earth, and we have misrepresented or omitted key details. We have been remiss not only on the story side but also in terms of communicating this story in ways that bring life change and invite others to follow Jesus. As we saw in the last chapter, most Jesus-followers will never see anyone respond to their invitation to come to Jesus. Something seems skewed here, considering that Jesus' main mandate in Matthew 28 was, "As you go, make disciples." The solution to our ineffectiveness can't simply be a better *method*. We have tried methodological alterations, and the results are no different. What if the *story* we are telling needs to be examined?

Gospel Lite

The story many evangelical pastors tell from the pulpit—the one that many pastors learned in conservative seminaries—and the story many of us therefore use to "share our faith" (the old word would be *evangelize*) is that "you are broken, messed up, heading to hell—and you need a fix." The story continues: Jesus has come and lived a perfect life, so that when he died, he could die the death you should have died. If you will trust him and his death, you can now live the life he lives and someday have a seat forever with him in eternity. For all of our obsession with getting people seats in heaven, it's amazing that this didn't seem to be a big agenda item for Jesus. If it had been a high priority, you would have heard Jesus talking about how to get to heaven, what prayers to say to get to heaven, doing miracles as attention getters that would open the door for him to do the real ministry of helping people secure seats in the afterlife. But Jesus didn't do this. I don't remember a single time he did a miracle for the purpose of getting to the "real important issue" of that person's eternal condition.

This observation continues to be greeted with strong reactions, but the reactions seem to be primarily emotional because this version of the story is so deeply entrenched. Conference to conference, pastor to pastor, Jesus-follower to Jesus-follower, the negative responses, when they have come, have by and large been emotional push-backs rather than well-reasoned criticisms of textual interpretations of the biblical text.

We have been telling a thin-slice, propositionalized, low-calorie version of the real story, and this approach is in keeping with our modern love affair with *information*. Here is precisely the hint we need to pay attention to: How much of the story we tell is influenced by the modern container we are in?

Here is the summary in proposition form that has given rise to a whole methodology:

- You are a sinner and separated from God (spiritually dead).

- You need a remedy for your condition—a remedy you cannot provide.

- God loves you so much he wants to be in relationship with you, but he is so offended by your sin that he can't.

- God has provided a payment for your sin, which will at the same time take care of his offense at your sin.

- God the Father sent Jesus, his Son, who lived a perfect life, thereby perfectly performing where we have miserably failed.

- Jesus dies a death we should have died.

- If you accept what Jesus did for you and make it your own, you can be in relationship with God the Father and Jesus. You typically do this through a "sinner's prayer," where you can mark a decisive date and turning point for your conversion.

Now there may be omitted parts in certain renditions, and there may be some necessary expansions and amplified details, but the above propositions quite fairly and accurately represent the evangelical message that many of us have spent much of our ministry making known. I would be included in that group—and so would Betty Sue. She felt uneasy early on in our classes as we were talking about this very issue. But it was at this point that she could so clearly identify with her upbringing and the story line she knew. While her reactions at times were spirited, she so badly wanted to enter spiritual conversations with friends and family members—and even her real estate clients—that she simply couldn't help keeping her ears open.

The Gospel According to Jesus

Here is the rub: Did Jesus go around offering the propositional distillation we just noted? Was this what constituted following him? Jesus, it seems, had a fundamentally different understanding of his mission. He wanted to broker shalom. Jesus was interested in imparting wholeness to people, and while eternity in fellowship with him is in fact a part of that wholeness, it wasn't a primary part of the conversation he had with people.

This isn't interpretive hocus-pocus; it is simply reading the gospel narratives and trying to note the conversational topics Jesus dealt with. I think we also need a heightened realization that Jesus came and spoke in the context of an already unfolding story, a story in which he had a role — a culminative role. I can't over-state this: *Jesus came on the scene when the stage had been perfectly set for his entrance* (see Galatians 4). He was part of a story that had been underway for hundreds and hundreds of years. Without an understanding of the basic contours of this story, we will never really understand why Jesus did come. And in the absence of that understanding, we will create abbreviations and shorthands to muddle our way through. In the process we will botch the story and empty it of its power.

I wonder if part of our problem in being able to grasp that Jesus is part of a longtime horizon that has all sorts of story and plot tension in it is that most of us have little sense of our own historical timeline *and* little, if any, sense that we too are part of an unfolding narrative. Most of us simply don't have generations and generations of stories we can pass down to our next kids. We might conjure up some stories about great-grandma and grandpa, but that would be about it for most of us. To have guiding stories stretching back a millennium and bringing meaning and historical context to our lives — that would be unheard-of.

Against this narrative-rich backdrop and broad time horizon Jesus entered human history. Without a sense of this elegant plot and story line, we are severely handicapped in retelling the narrative and using its contours to help others find wholeness in the midst of their personal fragmentation. Let's look at some broad brushstrokes.

The Stage and Story Line

The Old Testament has a number of stories that serve as overarching frameworks or important reference points by which almost everything else in Israel's story is guided. The role of *the creation story* has already been mentioned and will be explored at length in another part of this chapter. Three other stories direct much of Israel's self-understanding.[1]

- *The exodus story.* The opening books of the Old Testament (the Torah) have this story in the very center of their lens. The exodus is a story of journey and movement—a movement from slavery to freedom because of God's choice to love and to bring wholeness. The Torah is largely about the exodus and what follows when a people are called by God out of slavery.

- *The exile story.* This is the context into which Jesus entered as he came to this earth. In this situation John the Baptist burst onto the scene in the desert and by the Jordan River. Both of these geographical notes in the Gospels hold enormous symbolism for the telling of Israel's story. The exile, too, is a story of journey, process, and discovery and can be characterized as a story of movement from marginalization to restoration, from brokenness to wholeness. Israel's prophets give voice to this story and the substories that comprise it. These, too, were a powerful shaping force in Israel's self-understanding.

- *The sacrificial system story.* This is the story of priestly mediation to keep people clean and worthy to offer worship. This is not primarily a story of journey, like the exodus and exile narratives, but rather of transaction. The Levitical laws and the purity and holiness codes were intended to keep

Israel pure before God, to describe what constitutes clean and unclean: "If you are unclean, this is what you can and cannot do. And if you are unclean and want to participate in worship, here is the price that must be paid."

These three stories form the core of Israel's narrative and corporate self-understanding. They tell her why she is, where she is from, on what she can hope—and about the God who first loved her and on whom she puts her hope in the midst of exile. Narrative contours such as these point out something I'll come back to: the Old and New Testaments give us a "larger than our own little lives" story into which our piece can fit and be shaped.

Jesus entered Israel's story with these three big pieces in her history, defining *who* she was and *why* she was. This is the ever-present backdrop into which John the Baptist came. This is the story line into which Jesus, in the fullness of time, was inserted. Without a sense of this story and the Jewishness of Jesus, we will end up thinking and talking as though Jesus dropped from heaven at a random place and time.

Against this specific backdrop Jesus starts his ministry with an important reading from Isaiah 61. Many of us today are so unfamiliar with the Old Testament that we struggle to reflect in our reading the sense the original hearers must have had, knowing the massive critical moment their historical story was approaching. Without understanding the narrative prior to Jesus' arrival, we are bound to abridge the story.

Jesus' Personal Mission Statement

I wonder what Jesus would tell us if we could ask him to share his "personal mission statement." It would be intriguing to know what Jesus thought about why he had come to earth. In the absence of a clear statement labeled by Jesus as "my personal mission," we can only inductively read what he said and did and then deduce what he thought he had come to do. There are several Scripture passages that provide key material statements made by Jesus. John 10:10 seems to be a candidate: "I have come that they may have life, and have it to the full." Another is found in the gospel of Luke:

> [Jesus] went to Nazareth, where he had been brought up, and on the Sabbath day he went into the synagogue, as was his custom. He stood up to read, and the scroll of the prophet Isaiah was handed to him. Unrolling it, he found the place where it is written:
>
>> "The Spirit of the Lord is on me,
>>> because he has anointed me
>>> to proclaim good news to the poor.
>> He has sent me to proclaim freedom for the prisoners
>>> and recovery of sight for the blind,
>> to set the oppressed free,
>>> to proclaim the year of the Lord's favor."
>
> Then he rolled up the scroll, gave it back to the attendant and sat down. The eyes of everyone in the synagogue were fastened on him. He began by saying to them, "Today this scripture is fulfilled in your hearing."
>
> Luke 4:16–21

Jesus is referring to the Isaiah 61 passage he has just read. To return to the framing stories of exodus, exile, and sacrificial system, what stories seem to get airspace here? Of the three primary stories that shape Israel's self-understanding, which one seems to be in the forefront as Jesus reads this section of Isaiah 61? Look at each line and ask, "Is this an exodus, exile, or sacrificial system action?"

There can be no doubt that Jesus brought exodus elements. The theme of freedom from slavery is clear enough in the above lines. The same could be said for the exile theme. The theme of release from the margins or fringes of exile to restoration and reconnection seems clear enough as well. This is shalom alive and in practice, up close and personal.

In every line Jesus utters he makes either exodus or exile statements. Absent are any aspects of the sacrificial or priestly story. In other words, as Jesus offers this statement, he is identifying his self-understanding with the role of being the facilitator of a new exodus or the restorer from exile. Does this mean Jesus isn't also the great sacrifice or the great high priest? Of course not. This image is explored later in the New Testament, for instance, in the book of Hebrews. When looking at Luke 4:16–21 and comparing it with Jesus' conversations and actions, it is clear that exodus and exile get primary and nearly exclusive airplay. The construction of Luke's gospel makes this speech no small matter. It becomes a jumping-off point for the way in which Luke designs the narratives that follow.

Reading this Luke 4 passage should help us recalibrate our thinking about what Jesus came to bring and do. But many of us are so deeply entrenched in one particular way of reading the Gospels and thinking we know why Jesus came that we tend to reread these exodus and exile announcements through a spiritualizing lens and mute them of any actual, physical, real-life meaning. In other words, we see Jesus as saying not that he came to make blind eyes see, but that he came to make spiritually blind eyes see spiritual truth. Do we really have the right to inject this into this passage at this point?

I recently attended a conference where we read the Luke 4 passage and then quickly looked at what Jesus is recorded as doing in the following chapters of Luke's gospel. Go take a look. Our knee-jerk tendency when we read this passage is to spiritualize it. We are able to consistently make these Luke 4 statements reflect spiritual conditions instead of the obvious physical realities they narrate. For example, "the poor" are those who are poor in spirit, and the "good news" is about how to get to heaven and be reconciled to God (especially important to the poor because they have nothing here and now, so we reason). The "freedom" proclaimed to the prisoners is about freedom from the spiritual bondage and prison of sin. The "recovery of sight" for the blind is about those who are spiritually blind and who need to see the light of Jesus. We have become master spiritualizers.

I make this judgment because I repeatedly run into people who, when reading this passage, interpret it this way—and it's not just people in the pew who do this; trained pastors in the pulpit seem to share this nearly universal reading. When I challenge this reading, people inevitably say, "Well, yeah, I get that Jesus said it that way to connect with people, but obviously he meant something far more important and deeper than just helping poor people out of their poverty or helping blind people see. Jesus was about eternity, which is why he died, right?"

Do you see the problem that Christianity (at least the conservative evangelical flavor) faces? The conversation I recounted above I have had dozens of times. And invariably I get a circular reasoning response: "I know that Jesus came to get people into heaven, so I know when he talks about other human needs, he must really be talking about some sort of *spiritual need*. And I know that spiritual need is eternity, because Jesus' mission was to talk about and get people into eternity." So our preconceived ideas cause us to misread the text so that we confirm our preconceived ideas.

But it is likely Jesus really *did* know what he was doing. He knew how to talk about spiritual things when he wanted to and physical things when he wanted to. Maybe the reality is precisely the opposite of what we have been taught. What if Jesus came to address human need, to bring shalom, to dole out free "pink spoon" samples—and in the process have people join his family, a family that lives together in harmony and love? Is it possible our whole construal of salvation is so otherworldly that we don't know how to read the text honestly and as a result aren't sure how to help the world?

When we read Luke 4 and then pause and read what follows, something quite disruptive emerges. The spiritual "How can I get to heaven" interpretation is nowhere to be found:

- 4:33–35 While in the synagogue, Jesus heals a demon-possessed man.
- 4:36–37 Summary of people's amazement and how news about Jesus spread
- 4:38–39 Jesus heals a woman with a high fever
- 4:40–41 Summary of Jesus' healing of all who came to him with various diseases
- 5:12–14 Jesus heals a man with leprosy
- 5:15 Summary of how news about Jesus' works spread

Though I'm willing to go through chapter after chapter of the Gospels, there is no need to—the pattern and content are quite clear, and you know how to read. Jesus balanced his preaching ministry with a strong demonstration of *doing*—just as he said he would in Luke 4. And the kinds of things he did were physical and miraculous and were not primarily about showing us how to get to eternity. I know it is hard to hear this and to fit it into our preconceived cubbyholes, but if we read the text with clear minds, we will have trouble coming to any other conclusion.

If there was ever a good time for Jesus to engage people in the "Where are you going when you die?" conversation, it seems it would have been immediately after he performed a miracle for them. I suspect that a leper will pretty much sit and listen to anything you have to say if you've just healed him from the kind of horrible condition that put him on the fringes of society and left him and his family as permanent social outcasts, unable to get a job, go to worship, or shop in the marketplace. But Jesus never had that conversation. He was content to touch this man, make him whole, and see him restored to the community—with no further conversation about anything.

Not an Owner's Manual

In our modern world it is exactly this narrative that we have given up. We have been co-opted by the game rules of the modern world and have reduced the Bible to a set of propositional principles to apply. We even call it an "owner's manual for life." If we simply propositionalize the message of the Bible, we violate the main contribution it can make in providing a cohesive narrative story line that sets Christianity apart from other world religions. Most religions think we should help others, love our neighbors, be self-controlled, and kind—and so does Christianity. But this isn't the unique contribution to the conversation.

The reduction of God's big fat story down to a set of executable to-dos is problematic for another, even more substantial reason. While the church is quick to *say* we are all about grace, when I listen to preaching and Bible studies, I am not so convinced that we really practice what we preach. I think, "Mission Control, we have a problem."

We have taken the Bible as a large, sweeping, elegant narrative and spliced it down to individual moral anecdotes. We study the individual stories, largely disconnected from their context, and then we pull out "the truth to live by." Let me ask you, when was the last time you heard the Zacchaeus narrative of Luke 19 preached within its context? The fact that most of us don't even know the context is proof positive of the very issue I raise. Whatever we think the story of Zach is about, it is rarely read against the backdrop of the preceding story and in the context of setting up the subsequent story. The splicing of these broader blocks of story, however, has serious implications.

If we look only at the individual stories of Luke 19, we see four different story units most of us have heard—as individual stories. Few of us in our own personal Bible study (or in a study led by someone else) have asked why these stories are strung together by Luke in this context. This slicing of this chapter into little story units, while fine for examining the small units by themselves, ends up missing the whole point of the chapter if they are never put back together again. The Zach story is about a tax collector who experiences salvation due to a business ethics epiphany. His inclusion in the family is a point of surprise in the text because tax collectors are part of the "out" group. They are not part of the family "in" crowd. Zach's conversion is therefore a surprise in the story: someone who was thought to be "out" is "in"!

The next story unit about the ten minas is a fascinating narrative on the heels of the Zach story. While this passage is usually the focus of sermons during stewardship Sundays or in a financial giving series, with little regard for its context, it has little to do with stewardship of the financial sort. This story unit has many important details that serve to frame it (notably the authorial comment made in verse 11 and the concluding death sentence made by Jesus in verse 26). The story is about a group of people who thought they were "in." They were doing their duty to what they deemed was the best of their ability, but in the end they were found to be "out," not "in." The concluding framing comment made by Jesus in verse 26 makes it clear the story isn't about giving money or using your spiritual gifts in your local church. Not even close. This story is about the smug folks who thought they had it all figured out but happened to be dead wrong.

The Zach story is about a guy who most people thought was "out" but in fact wasn't. The story of the minas was about a group most people thought was "in" but in fact wasn't. The stories juxtapose the "who is in and who is out" assumptions. When these stories are followed by the Palm Sunday narrative, it may not immediately dawn on us why all of these stories have been pieced together here. Jesus' comment in verse 27 about the characters in his story not wanting a king are the setup to the triumphal entry narrative — what is known as the "coming of the king." When this narrative is followed by one of the harshest judgment stories against Israel and Jerusalem in all of the gospel narratives, namely, Jesus' clearing of the temple,[2] we see an intentional design to Luke's story arrangement. In biblical studies we call this "composition criticism."

Luke 19 stands as a great example of how the deconstruction of a chapter into smaller story units can lead to a misunderstanding of the author's reason for including them in the first place. So what is the application? The same principle illustrated here applies to even larger blocks of biblical text. If this happens at the small Luke 19 scale, what about the whole of Luke's gospel? What about the whole of the four gospels in the flow of the New Testament? What about the various units in the Old Testament—such as the Law, the Writings, and the Prophets—that Jesus refers to? How do the broader contours of the narrative tell a different story from the little fragmented stories out of which we extract morals for cute applications? This is the challenge we face in constructing—or, more accurately, reconstructing—the overarching biblical story. For it is in the big story that we will find the power to transform life.

Does this mean we should never study small blocks of the biblical text? Does this mean using methods such as *lectio divina* to reflect on individual verses is inappropriate? I would never suggest this. But I fear we have dissected things and have had modeled an atomizing approach to the Bible so often that we have little understanding of the broad brushstrokes and how the units fit together. We could never understand any other written story if we simply took random lines from random chapters day in and day out. The story would never be able to come together for us.

Picking up on Plato's contention that all religious frameworks are comprised of two dimensions—*logos* and *mythos*—author Karen Armstrong draws important conclusions that may provide clues for our next steps. In this framework, *logos* is the word, proposition, rules, doctrines, systems of religion—all of those things that go into formal structure and dogma. *Mythos*, on the other hand, has to do with spirit, power, the transformational character of narrative, mystery, and transcendence. Armstrong observes that any time we have a collapse of *mythos* (the power of the story) into *logos* (rules), we end up with fundamentalism—and not just Christian fundamentalism but all kinds of fundamentalism. The collapse of *mythos* into *logos* happens whenever rules become more important than the power of the story to transform and whenever propositions trump the compelling spirit of the story that embeds these propositions. We need both of these. But that is exactly the point: *we need both.*

Armstrong argues that our emphasis on the *logos* component and minimizing of the *mythos* dimension is a distinctively modern issue and one of the main reasons that without a re-thought, re-storied Christianity we will be relegated even further to the margins.[3] I wonder if much of evangelical Christianity isn't, in fact, very slim on *mythos* and blindly addicted to *logos* supremacy. This is, I know, a harsh suggestion, but we need to consider our practice. Do we give people proposition-full messages on Sunday morning, or do we invite them into a reshaping of their story in view of the biblical one? Are we trying to get people to conform to a set standard out there, as defined by the "biblical rules," or are we inviting them to reconsider the story line that gets them up in the morning? Certainly the way we have labeled the "problem" (you are a sinner) and shared the "solution" (Jesus came and died for you) seems to point to an addiction to *logos* supremacy.

The Grand Narrative

Where does this idea of *wholeness* or *wellness* originate? And where does our desire for it come from? It seems like a stupid question, doesn't it? Everyone has a default setting—a built-in yearning for shalom, for wellness, for wholeness.

When we understand the entire story, starting with creation rather than the fall, we start with God's intended purposes for the world. When we start with creation, we start with the very reasons we exist and the basis of our yearnings. When we understand creation, we have a clear picture of what the whole world is heading back toward as all things are ultimately restored in Jesus.[4] I suggest that unless we understand God's plan and story in creation, we will be less than clear about his restoration plans and hopes.

Mininarratives

Let's develop this idea that we must start the story in the beginning, which would be Genesis 1, not Genesis 3. I've already noted that the typical shorthand for the common evangelical message has been fall-redemption (i.e., humanity is fallen and needs to be redeemed). The typical person in our postmodern culture has no resonance about his or her fallen condition. Unfortunately, the extent of our creativity in helping others connect to this "fallen condition" has been to repeat the same story over and over, increasing the volume a bit more each time.

Our storytelling paralysis is where we have missed the boat. Many of us hold an implicit assumption that there is one, and only one, correct story of Jesus and the cross, but even a cursory look at the New Testament shows that those who put the biblical canon together thought we needed at least four versions of the story. And it doesn't stop there. Theologian James McClendon Jr. says there were various stories of why Jesus died and what it means to humanity:

> To the question why the cross? The right story, rightly told, is the right answer.... Yet the "right story" seems to beg the question. Granting the necessity for narrative, which is the "right story"? From many gospels, ancient Christianity selected four, not one. And when we recover the narrative shape of the later "theories" of atonement, we find conflicting narratives. *Which* story is adequate?... Irenaeus and Gregory with

their conflict and ransom plots, Anselm and Calvin with their tales of a quest for divine satisfaction, Abelard and Moberly and Bushnell with their psychologizing analyses of a costly inner journey—all posit atonement narratives.[5]

McClendon articulates all of this in the context of the tremendous interpretive creativity shared by both Christian and Jewish rabbinic history. The point of all this is to help us come to grips with the fact that there is not simply one right version of the story. Story and narrative by definition are able to bear layers of meaning, perspectives on these meanings, and various viewpoints of meaning. This isn't a plea for the text to mean anything we want it to mean, thereby rendering it meaningless; it is rather a plea for intellectual humility about the certainty of our version of the story being the only or most accurate version.[6]

I want to suggest that if God had wanted everything in neat, unmistakable, propositional form, he was more than able to deliver that. For example, most of the book of Proverbs comes in that very form. Narrative by its very genre is more complex and perspectival. In other words, the person(s) you identify with on any given reading causes the "truth" of the narrative to be felt in very different ways. Read the healing of the paralyzed man in Mark 2 from the perspective of Jesus, then from the perspective of the paralyzed man, and finally from the perspective of the Pharisees. What you feel and see will be very different, based on your changed perspective.

Saying all of this doesn't mean that each person isn't in need of the salvation life Jesus came to bring. It does mean that if the only way we can retell the story is by making it fit as an answer to our constructed problem and solution ("you are a sinner; Jesus came and died for you"), then we are narrowing and misrepresenting the narrative. We cannot continue to handle the text in ways that force it into a flatland terrain where there are no differing vantage points. Could it be that this is one of the reasons many of us struggle so intensely with effectively engaging outsiders in spiritual conversations?

I just love this statement that comes out of systems thinking: *Your current system is perfectly designed to get the current results you are getting.* The popularized version may be better known: *If you always do what you've always done, you will always get what you have always gotten.* Our results demonstrate that we are not connecting—and I think it is because we are telling a Story*Lite* version of the full and rich story.

Mini, Micro, Meta — What's the Big Deal?

I continued to be motivated by my enthusiastic conversations with church people about this abbreviated story. There seems to be such interest in rethinking an area we assumed we had figured out. When we reduce the big, fat biblical narrative to a set of propositions that fix the eternal-destiny problem of humanity, we have emptied the narrative of being, well—*narrative.* And when we no longer have a narrative but an instruction manual for life, we are missing the power of the story at just the juncture our culture most needs it.

One of the interesting conversations that has been going on in the area of postmodernism is the loss of what is called a "metanarrative." Metanarrative is simply a fancy word for an overarching story line that makes sense of the separated fractions of our existence on this planet. The French philosopher Jean-François Lyotard observes that "postmodernism is what happens when master stories lose their appeal and become incredible."[7] In this postmodern world, philosophers and literary critics tell us, we live in the ruins of our collapsed grand narratives and simply buy time as we tell our own little disconnected stories, our own "singular tales," as Lyotard calls them.

Since modernity makes the person, rather than God, the creator of his or her own personal world, the world no longer has a legitimating authority or reason for being. The disappointment of modernity is that the grand narrative for a better world through progress and technological breakthrough simply hasn't happened. Knowing this, though it may seem a bit arcane or academic, allows us to see why spiritual conversation is so important and prevalent and why a retelling of the *whole* Christian story, not the abbreviated modern propositionalized version, is so critical.[8]

The often-expressed postmodern angst is that whoever writes the metanarrative has the power, and the typical postmodern is not about to be dominated by an external power. Therefore, the argument goes, postmodernism is about the dissolving of any sort of metanarrative. You can see, then, why Christianity is suspect when it comes to the metanarrative we claim to export to the world: "You are a sinner, and Jesus came and died for you." Do you see how the typical person in our postmodern context hears this? The opening "you are a sinner" is an enormous statement of power. We are judging someone else by some standard they aren't even aware of and probably don't buy. This is the ultimate power move. Couple that with militant evangelism language — "win them over" and "evangelistic crusade" — and it's no wonder people often tune us out.

Can you see, though, how this is a golden opportunity for the full Christian narrative to have a voice? Yet it will never have a voice if we reduce it to a bunch of disconnected little stories we tell and then extract a moral. The *grand narrative* of the Bible is different from that of other metanarratives, which so many postmoderns feel are about power, control, and oppression. Jesus' death and sacrifice make it the *anti-power* narrative and the premier example of downward mobility. Jesus provides the model of how a story gives life cohesion and coherence without the attending domination and control themes that inform much of today's ideology.

What happens to my life when there is no metanarrative into which the little vignettes of my life fit? Without an overarching story, there is no plot tension, no direction, no trajectory, no purpose. At best, purpose is personally constructed and individually defined. Life then takes on highly personalized meanings and purposes, but most of them are cut off from any overarching story that would bring a sense of coherence to a person's life. It's easy to see, then, that individual personal stories become "all about me" because nothing else can overarch "me" to make sense of it all.

Beyond Us

Narrative is one area in which Christianity makes a monumental contribution to life and to the postmodern conversation. Not only do we feel we have a story—an overarching story into which our personal narratives fit and make sense—but the overarching story *isn't* one of domination and control. The essence of the Christian story is that of selfless service, love, compassion, and care. Coercion, control, and power are not part of the equation. Sadly, the Christian church hasn't always lived out her story this way, but it is her story nonetheless.

All major religions—Confucianism, Buddhism, Islam, Hinduism, and so on—have some attachment to a unique founder. Not all claim the sorts of things that we claim about Jesus, but the fact that most world religions have a unique founder is pretty clear. I want to suggest that while Jesus *is* unique, this viewpoint will not be met with huge applause, let alone affirmation, by those outside the Christian faith. Other gods have claimed virgin birth, miraculous powers, resurrection, and so forth.

What if our elevation of the uniqueness of Jesus has actually short-circuited conversation? What if there is another place to start the conversation that would find resonance? What if the very way we have been designed and crafted by God causes us to want our personal narratives to have cohesion? And what if one of the central and unique contributions of Christianity is an overarching, make-sense-of-it-all narrative? We need to do far more reflection on piecing together this make-sense-of-it-all biblical story and helping Christ-followers understand and communicate it if we want to carry on intelligent and informed spiritual conversations in our pluralistic and globalized world.

What is the overarching story and trajectory of Islam or Buddhism, or Hinduism or Confucianism? Take a few minutes to sketch out their story. Hard-pressed? Floundering? Unclear? No wonder. However you define each of these religions, you likely won't find an overarching story that makes sense of human history and the role the human narrative plays in it. One of the distinctive Christian claims is that from the beginning to end of human history, we have been invited to play an integral and unfolding role. I am *not* saying other religions may not have their own creation narratives; they do. I am *not* saying they don't try to provide an ethical framework for life; they do. But the Christian metanarrative—into which people can integrate their own fractured and broken narratives to find shalom and wholeness—is the very thing people are looking and longing for. Most people I know have an intuitive sense that there should be some reason for their "being," some purpose as to why they are here on the planet. I think the Christian church has the narrative that people are looking for. The question is, will we tell *that* story?

■

"Ron," Betty Sue said as she began to wrap up our conversation, "everything I've been learning about the big story became so obvious to me this week when I was showing a house to an Indian couple. They were new to our area. He was a schoolteacher, and she had a part-time nutrition business in their home. What was really interesting was they told me they want to know about churches and temples in the area. Those were their exact words — "churches and temples in the area." So I admit I was a bit bewildered by that one. I probed a bit and asked what kind of churches and temples they were looking for. They confided that they were Hindu by culture but not practicing in any sort of religious way, and while they would always be Hindu, they were looking for a church or temple that would help them *make sense of their lives.* They felt they and their kids needed that!"

"So, Betty Sue, what did you tell them?" I asked.

"We ended up going to lunch to talk about what they meant by 'make sense of our lives.' And for two hours we talked about how life is a story and how there must be something out there to make sense of our story. It was so exciting to see how all I've been learning provided such a great backdrop for me to think in broader, more helpful ways."

CHAPTER 3

The Human Text

Darrell is a dear friend. We have engaged in sports together, been in each other's homes, shared meals, and talked about spiritual things, but I know of no one more engaged in and determined to live the American Dream. His cell phone beeps with investment portfolio updates four times a day. Investments are currently being monitored for profits to purchase the *next* boat and Jet Ski. Debt is crazy-high because the beachfront house was a must-have, as were the his and hers convertibles they bought when they moved in. "None of this is keeping up with the Joneses," Darrell assures me. "It's just living the good life, and that's what it's all about, right?" All his frat buddies check in monthly to see how everyone is doing financially. Seriously! It's almost like a competition. But it's not like they got out of school two years ago. Darrell is thirty-eight.

Darrell and I have talked a lot about spiritual things and spiritual values. But the American Dream's allure—and its supposed promise—is so powerful that it is the driver of most decisions. "Ron," he told me, "I'm not a materialist. I simply want the good things for me and my family. Working hard, even going into debt for it, isn't a problem. Living the kind of life I can live here in America is part of my right to pursue freedom and happiness."

Welcome to the third component—the *human text*, or human story. The *biblical* text has to be intelligible in the *cultural context* in which we are called to do ministry. It is in this context that the *human text* or story is shaped. The text we live and the shape of our story are functions of our personal experiences and the contexts into which we have been born. In the absence of a genuine overarching narrative to really make sense of life, it seems we have had to find a substitute. In the absence of a compelling religious story, we will find something to make sense of our lives. Often the answer comes in the form of the American Dream.

The postmodern conversation has much about it that we should leverage for the spiritual conversation landscape. The deconstruction of the metanarrative that has emerged in our post-Enlightenment modern world is something for which we in the Christian church should be thankful.

The American Dream World

The American Dream has been written about and discussed at length and has been celebrated and vilified. But its visceral presence betrays that it is much more than a nice idea. The narrative tension and plot provided by the American Dream are just what many people need to get motivated every morning. This is the story line that inevitably shapes, molds, and influences the human text—our human lives—whether we are aware of it or not. Our ability to enter into spiritual conversations with grace and insight makes understanding the human condition important. The human condition of which I speak isn't simply the "everyone needs God" condition. But the specific conditions of our personal stories—

with all our pursuits, dreams, hopes, and fears—are molded by the context in which we live.

We are encouraged to buy into an awful lot in the name of the American Dream. Some version of the dream plays out in the heads of most of us in the United States, starting at a very early age. You are supposed to go to school, get a good degree, possibly get into a grad school, get a great job making big money, find the ideal spouse (but not at too young an age), have kids who are near-perfect angels and who attend preschool at two-and-a-half years old because they show Mensa potential, find a gorgeous home, and raise a well-adjusted family while one or both parents climb the corporate ladder to support the perfect lifestyle complete with exotic trips and all the toys. Out of breath? I thought so. And if there is time and money left after all that, "Oh, yeah—let's help some others out if possible."

While this is the American Dream sketched out in advertising, television shows, magazines, and movies, it is a dream realized by very, very few, even though the pursuit seems to cross ethnic, socioeconomic, and educational lines. I recently talked to an Iraqi man who came to the United States with the hope of buying a house, sending his kids to college, becoming a citizen, and making a better life for the next generation by starting his own business. His parting shot to me was, "That is the American Dream, isn't it?"

While my characterization may be a bit overdramatic, I am afraid something like this rolls around in the heads of many people in the United States as an—or even *the*—American ideal. One of my dearest friends recently told me about a new business venture he is entertaining. He had met two Hispanic guys who crossed the border in Arizona looking for work. They had been painting houses for the last several years just to make ends meet. And they came to America why? Their own words: "We can realize the American Dream here." They have now started their own nutrition business and made $32,000 last month. I could give illustration after illustration showing that the Dream isn't just a white middle-class hope. It motivates people far and wide who come from wildly diverse backgrounds.

Somehow, someway we are slowly but surely being told various versions of this story—and we bite into it, chew it up, and swallow it. It is assimilated into our bloodstream, and like a latent virus, it remains quietly but powerfully resident in every cell of our being. It is a pervasive part of our existence, but we are almost completely blind to its presence.

My friend Mike recently told me about an East Coast friend whose daughter was heading off to college. Mike asked him what she was going to study, and his friend—in a tone of frustration—mentioned the profession. Mike asked him why the frustration. His friend's response? "Do you know what the annual income is for that, Mike?" Mike said he didn't. And his friend said, "$35,000 a year." Mike's friend went on to say that if she wasn't going to do something more lucrative, he wasn't paying for college. Mike was surprised by this response because his friend seemed to be so normal, regular, and nice. He didn't seem like some money-grubbing, dollars-motivated kind of guy. Many of us struggle with at least making sure we *appear* to be living the American Dream—which can even be done vicariously through our kids.

I realize this is only one example, but surely not an isolated one. What is Mr. East Coast saying to his daughter, who has a great profession in mind—one that is in line with her passions and one that would be a huge asset to a community, even though making big bucks is not part of the equation? What is he saying to her? What is he saying to my friend Mike? Isn't he saying that making money is more important than finding your gifts and using them to serve the world? Is he convinced that living the American Dream is better than aligning with one's purpose and passion? This is one example of the American Dream holding sway in not-so-subtle ways. Recognizing just a bit about how this is propagated may help us realize how to enter into people's personal narratives.

Creating Unknown Needs

In 2001, Thomas H. Davenport and John C. Beck wrote a book called *The Attention Economy.* The book's essential idea is that marketers and advertisers need to capture your attention for a brief period of time in the hope that you'll recognize a need you want filled or a need you didn't know you had. Their basic thesis? *Attention is scarce.* What gets your attention will grow in your mind; and if it grows in your mind long enough, you will act on it. We live in a time when marketers are trying to manage our attention.[1]

When was the first time you saw a commercial for little gel strips you can place on your teeth to make them whiter? Is this something that has been around for the last fifty years? Nope. The technology is now available, so millions of dollars in advertising are spent trying to convince people that their teeth are yellower than they should be and that they need to spend $24.99 to have whiter chompers. What gets attention grows. Sure enough, you bombard people long enough, and what wasn't a thought becomes a thought; and a thought given attention becomes a need, and a need attended to becomes a purchase. Crest Whitestrips are only one minor example. But add to the plotline the tensions of house size, car type, vacation kind, and a host of other things, and the narrative tension is enough to keep people busy for an entire lifetime.

So many things go into the pressure exerted by a need to live the dream. The compilation of these things end up molding and shaping our human spirit, our human aspirations, our hope for a better tomorrow. And this is exactly why understanding all three texts is so important. The context is the arena in which the human text is infused. The context is the container that marinates the human story. *Infuse* and *marinate* are the right metaphors — because both speak of an influence that is slow, quiet, imperceptible at first, but all-pervasive in the end.

Pervasive and Subversive

I don't know about you, but when I do an interior gut check, I almost always compare myself with those who have more — and saying *almost always* may be generous. I make these mental comparisons because I am prompted — no, bombarded — in every store I walk into, in every advertisement and magazine cover I see, by the message that I *lack*. My skin isn't smooth enough, my house isn't "smart enough," I don't have the right clothes, I don't eat organic, I have the wrong vacuum cleaner, I use an inferior dishwashing detergent, I sit on out-of-date furniture, and I apply less than adequate hair color coverage to conceal my gray. I recognize that advertising all too often creates a false and unfulfilling narrative tension in my spirit that can drive unhealthy behavior. The whole system is set up to tell me that I am less than I can and should be — and here is how I can remedy that lack.

Having been a pastor, I can tell you that pastors and churches are no exception. When I was a pastor, the needs to "pull off the show," "grow the congregation numerically," "keep the budget expanding to do kingdom work," sounded legit and noble, but the mixture of motives was hard to sort out, let alone keep straight. I remember well the first time it dawned on me that "my church" was one that a lot of people envied—I mean one that a lot of other pastors envied. There were guys who would have loved to be in my shoes. We were big and creative and were doing cutting-edge things; we had an enviable staff and an incredible ethos—and people were writing about us. And I can remember this cold feeling coming over me as I realized I was being co-opted by the "bigger is better" story. I was slowly being enculturated into "The American Dream: Church Edition." With big numbers, great creativity, ample budgets, and "coolest building" status comes bigger ego, bigger ego, and—yeah—bigger ego. I realize I live my life in community, but I am not responsible for others—only for my own life and heart. And I didn't like how I was being snared by the culture of "more is superior." It was influencing and molding my humanness; it was shaping my story. My human text was being hijacked by another author, and the power of that "author" was as pervasive as it was subversive.

I think the American Dream is as much a struggle for the church, the pastor, and every staff member as it is for anyone else in the world. I wonder if the reality of this struggle is why Jesus' statement that it is hard for the rich to enter the kingdom of God has such bite for those in the West today and why we dance around its clear implications so often.

The American Dream story line—or the Gerbil Wheel Tale, as I like to call it—is a reflexive response to a lack of perceived purpose and is nearly universal in America. The stranglehold of the American Dream narrative on the minds and lives of people is independent of economic or educational level. It has no respect for gender, age, or ethnicity. This story has no lack of religious adherents as well, whether Christian, Jewish, Muslim, or Hindu. The American Dream is as American and ubiquitous as McDonalds and Wal-Mart.

The universality of this dream is precisely what makes it so difficult to identify as a motivator of human life. The American Dream is quiet but powerful, an enormous daily motivator and yet hidden from our eyes because its presence is so obvious and accepted as the "way things are."

My sense is the American Dream is nothing but another variation on the gerbil wheel that spins and spins and spins and never stops. I didn't have any dogs or cats growing up, but I did go through the third-grade infatuation with rodents of various sorts. I admit it — I had a gerbil cage, complete with inverted water bottle and spinning torture wheel. I can hardly think of a better illustration for the American Dream than the gerbil wheel. Endless spinning, fast leg movements, and creative gymnastics to keep you interested in staying on the wheel, but when you get off for a moment, you realize you have gone nowhere. Maybe our obsession with treadmills in health clubs is a quiet indication of a larger condition.

My friend Chad has bought into the American Dream, but the truth is, so have I — and maybe you have too. I'm not saying that Chad is a wanton materialist, egocentric status seeker, or hardcore corporate ladder addict. I certainly don't think these words describe me either. I merely make the observation that many of us have bought into the prevailing story line, and it is a motivator in our day-to-day life. Pervasive and subversive. While there are all sorts of variations and nuances to the American Dream, the basic contours are beyond dispute.

All human lives are a story and lived out as a story. It just so happens that we in America are profoundly influenced by some hidden authors who have a huge influence in shaping our story line. Let's dig deeper into this idea of our lives as a narrative.

Living *Truman Show* Lives

Remember the movie *The Truman Show*? A full-blown story line of a 24/7 reality soap opera into which Jim Carrey's character, Truman Burbank, is inserted—with no clue that he is the star of the show? I wonder if Truman's total oblivion is not in some way a picture of our lives at times. The tagline of the movie was "All the world's a stage." We live on autopilot, unaware of what is moving us down the road, unaware that we are part of a world stage, trying to write the story of our human text.

We get up in the morning because we have decided life is worth living, and there is something about today that holds enough interest to motivate us to let our feet hit the floor. While this doesn't always happen consciously for the vast majority of us, it happens nonetheless, or else we would live lives of purposeless depression. An overarching narrative motivates all our lives, whether explicit or tacit. A grand story line, or what I've labeled a metanarrative, that brings cohesion, meaning, and purpose to our existence. What makes up this story line? Add together vocational aspirations, education, relationships, romance, children, and a steady stream of advertising, and you can start to see how a story emerges automatically, with no effort whatsoever. A grand narrative shapes up with time, and we find we are living with the challenges, crises, drives, promises, and possibilities that continue to pull us into the future. This sort of story keeps us interested and in the game, with no desire for exit—at least not yet. The challenge, of course, is that the motivations for each day are various and shifting and maybe—most of all for our conversation—tacit. In other words, our personal narratives have all the elements that move a story along, but most of these motivations for our narratives are quiet and subterranean.

As we grow in our understanding of the Gerbil Wheel Tale, we come to see not only the external motivations, such as pay raises or marketed items we think we need to make life good, but the deeper motivations within our hearts—motivations that seem to be in a different class. These internal motivators are a little less crass, brazen, and egocentric—at least they seem that way sometimes.

As we look on the inside, we find we have an architecture and design that yearns for transformation. But the drive for transformation gets muddied up and lost in cheap substitutes that drive our story to places that seem appealing at the moment but in the end are deeply disappointing.

Spiritual Conversation

We need to hear the story of the American Dream so we can get in touch with how its lure has worked on us and then how we can apply our insights to the arena of spiritual conversations.

The motivations, both in our lives and in every good story, are the things that create narrative tension and make the story interesting and engaging. This is true of all compelling stories, no matter what their format. Movies, fairy tales, and novels all have this narrative interest and tension. Without plot tension we put the book down or walk out of the movie. This plot tension can take the form of goals, desires, challenges, or tragedies; but no matter what it is, these tensions move the story along and keep readers and viewers interested long enough to see how it "all turns out."

Our lives aren't any different. We all have transformational architecture, these deep yearnings that motivate us on a day-to-day basis. This architecture of the human spirit seeks to find expression through the life of every human being. If we can come to understand this transformational architecture and how we have been designed by God, we may well find a common ground for conversation space. This is a core component of the human text. If we can understand this text, we will have the ability to enter into spiritual conversations naturally and with compelling interest.

What if the architecture of our hearts has been designed to seek satisfaction? What if the seeking of that satisfaction is what creates goals and challenges that make life interesting, demanding, engaging, and potentially exciting? Then we will find that the tension created by these goals and challenges moves us along as we seek resolution to the challenges of the plot or the goals in the story line.

We know what happens when life is void of tension. The absence of some sort of tension to move our narratives will create lives that make no sense and seem empty and thin. I've heard of extreme cases where the absence of healthy narrative tension led a person to choose destructive ways in a subliminal attempt to create narrative movement. These unhealthy avenues are in some cases about finding more excitement or thrills, more adrenaline, more ecstasy, more drama; in other cases they are about addiction, greater dependency, and more severe dysfunction. The common thread in all of this is the need for narrative tension so the story is worth engaging.

It is exactly the convergence of these universal transformational yearnings intersecting with an overarching narrative that brings spiritual conversation into focus. When we start to understand this architectural design in every human heart and how it interfaces with and empowers personal life narratives, we are hovering over the most important places where God is moving and where spiritual conversations are possible.

Splicing Our Lives Together

Consider how the American Dream is constructed. The things we think we need aren't things we've dreamed up on our own but the stuff that culture—advertisers, friends, teachers, television, movies, tabloids—tells us we need to have a full and exciting life, or to put it another way, a story line worth living for. But there is a problem. While we all have universal yearnings—yearnings architected into the very design of our hearts—this architecture has been tampered with. Much like the Tylenol tampering tragedy of 1982, the little capsules of deep-seated longings have been mixed with deadly cyanide. Unless checked, our infected yearnings will produce lives of frustration that ultimately reach a dead end—because consumerism creates never-ending dissatisfaction.

Because the American Dream has endless possibilities, to that degree it will never satisfy. We will always look toward the next chapter of our story, which we hope provides more excitement, a better office, a larger portfolio, a younger wife, a more talkative husband, a faster adrenaline rush, and more adventurous vacations. The never-ending litany is what keeps the tension going, the gerbil wheel spinning, until—until we get wise to the fact that it is, uhhhh, never-ending. Never-ending is simply another way of saying *never really satisfied*.

Some people will realize the American Dream in all its wanton splendor. The brother of my dear friend Ethan just called him to tell him he had landed the deal that will set him up for life so he'll never have a financial need again. Ethan's brother is in his early thirties. Ethan says his first response when he heard this news was fear for his brother. He said to me, "What happens when two years down the road his money has bought all there is to buy and there's no need of anything and he realizes that life is pretty boring and that the thrill of the hunt that drove him has evaporated. What then?" Will life make any sense for Ethan's brother, or will it all be just one plot tension resolved only to find the new plot tension of boredom even worse. When the plot tension of our personal narratives is informed primarily by the American Dream, we are in for a huge disappointment, even when it seems that we finally made it.

The challenge for those who live in America is to stand firm against marketing genius. We are challenged to face these questions: Will I become the author of my own life narrative and become yet another victim in the endless cycle of the Gerbil Wheel Tale? Or will I allow God to shape the contours of my story? Unless we start to understand how our personal narrative is being shaped by such forces, we may well continue on autopilot. When I can finally admit that overwhelming forces are being applied to shape my story—and when I realize that these forces strategically take advantage of the very transformational architecture God has put at the center of my being—then I'm beginning to recognize how my narrative gets quietly and powerfully shaped. This is the first step in being able to help anyone engage in spiritual conversations. If we are unable to live an alternative narrative, how can we possibly help others identify and then alter theirs?

I have no intention of blaming culture for our condition. It isn't culture's fault. Culture is a container. It can be used for good or evil; it can be helpful or not helpful.

While some people will "achieve" the American Dream, most won't—but they'll stay on the gerbil wheel and keep trying.

Instead of the American Dream realized, it will be the American Dream frustrated. And in our fragmented and often episodic life experiences, the idea of a continuity that brings some measure of order to our narrative is a relic of yesterday. In other words, we are contributing to a dissolving metanarrative; we are part of the reason there seems to be no overarching big fat story. Zygmunt Bauman, one of the brilliant sociologists of our time, writes:

> The collapse of long-term thinking, planning and acting, and the disappearance or weakening of social structures in which thinking, planning and acting could be inscribed for a long time to come, leads to a splicing of both political history and individual lives into a series of short-term projects and episodes which are in principle infinite, and do not combine into the kinds of sequences to which concepts like "development," "maturation," "career," or "progress" (all suggesting a preordained order of succession) could be meaningfully applied. A life so fragmented stimulates "lateral" rather than "vertical" orientations.[2]

Bauman's writing can be dense though insightful. If you need to stop and reread the above extract, go for it. Pretty depressing material, isn't it? That is exactly the point. This is a picture of where the human text is situated if there isn't a larger story into which it can fit. I think Bauman is on to something that may help us understand the human text as it is often lived out in day-to-day existence. Please note, I'm not questioning motives here. I think our personal narrative tension is never even thought about most of the time. We typically will let forces around us shape our lives. Awareness on this front takes vigilance and determination.

The Story Back in the Day

My parents, like most of my parents' friends, expected to live a small slice of the American Dream. They would all do the corporate thing for thirty to thirty-five years, take retirement on the pension that was well earned, and be role models in the community. They would be full-time grandparents, never missing a Little League game, soccer tournament, ballet recital, or anything their grandchildren were involved in.

Those days of the American Dream are long since over. The American Dream today looks very different and is no longer marked by the apparent stability of yesterday. Bauman's observation is poignant for our consideration when it comes to the issue of spiritual conversation. If our parents had a sense of "development," "maturation," "career," or "progress," to use Bauman's terms, then clearly we have moved to "splicing" together episodes and short-term projects in hopes of creating some coherence and meaning.

I am most fascinated by Bauman's conclusion in the quote above, though. Fragmented lives lead to the inability to have any sense of vertical orientation? Maybe it's because we're so consumed with the horizontal life. We constantly live in fear, wondering what catastrophe lurks in the next episode over which we have no control. In a generation that will have up to a half dozen or more career changes (contrast that with the situation back in the day), a post-9/11 consciousness, a volatile economy, and hostile global conditions—both on the geopolitical and ecological front—it is no wonder we live in an age of anxiety.

My hope for us in the remaining pages is that as we continue this journey through the land of spiritual conversations, we'll learn to listen carefully to what our culture provides us in terms of entry points for conversation, which is essentially what Paul did in Acts 17 in Athens. I also want to revisit a couple of the conversations I had with Chad, who has become a great golf buddy and a spiritual conversation partner. I have learned a lot from him as he has become increasingly aware of the transformational architecture rooted in his heart. He recognizes his core drive and desire, and he is on a journey of investigation.

Part 2

The Transformation

Transformation typically isn't instantaneous or haphazard. It requires intention and attention if the journey is to proceed. Because God has architected us with specific quests and yearnings, we have some hints about how this whole journey might unfold. We even have some clues about where there may be pitfalls to avoid. Spiritual conversations are for the express purpose of assisting with journey progress. Once we understand something of the context in which these conversations happen, we are ready to explore the storied nature of our lives and the narrative into which God invites us. Like all stories and narratives, however, the starting point, the opening scene of the story, is critical for understanding the rest of the plot and story line. When you change the opening chapter of a story, you are bound to change the trajectory and even the point of the story. Wouldn't it be something to realize that a story you had known your whole life actually started with a different opening chapter? While it may initially be a bit unnerving, it may be incredibly exciting and help make sense of parts of the story that never seemed to fit.

CHAPTER 4

Imago Dei

A small, slight woman with a weathered face and gnarled hands approached me one morning after my message at a church gathering in South Africa. Mandisa was a vineyard worker in the beautiful region of Stellenbosch. While she appeared to be a peasant, her near-perfect diction and eloquent speech showed she was more educated than first impressions indicated. She approached me with tears in her eyes. I hadn't ended my talk with a powerful closing illustration or gripping story, so I was perplexed about what might be going on inside of her.

"Mr. Ron, I have been connected to the dirt of this beautiful country my whole life. I touch the dirt, the leaves, the grapes, and the grass every single day. The sun beats down, and I get to smell all the different things God has created that go into the grapes we pick in the vineyard. It is hard work, but the creation of God—the mountains and rolling hills all around me—is pure joy for me."

Mandisa was glowing as she shared this, and she spoke in a quiet, almost reverent, tone.

"But what I have heard today brings me even greater joy. I

haven't thought about *me* coming from the dirt and being marked as unique, of having similarities with all the created world that I touch every day but also bearing in me a mark that makes me highly special. I have never thought about being God's reminder to the grapes and the grass and the dirt that I am from the same place they are but with one big difference: I am *imago dei*. I have a mark that makes me very, very different and infinitely valuable. I share a story with the dirt and the grapes and the grass, but my story has unique parts too. This will make me think different thoughts each day as I pick grapes and work in the dirt. I thank you, Mr. Ron."

Mandisa nodded her head gently, turned around, and walked away. My eyes, too, were full of tears.

"God Made Us" Narratives

As we learn about seeing our lives as narrative, it may be an obvious observation that God made us this way and that he made us unique and special in comparison to all other created things. We are made *imago dei*. This truth, as it grips a human spirit, has the power to transform. We may conclude that from the very beginning we have been made to be a part of a grand story, to gravitate toward compelling stories, and to be mesmerized by great storytelling. We may also conclude that, whether we know it or not, our lives are shaped and reshaped by narratives and story lines that often operate in ways that are nearly invisible but quietly present. In other words, whether we are fully aware or not, *our lives are storied*. Our lives gravitate toward narrative shape, and we will do all we can to make sure this shaping has at least some perceived value and meaning for us. We are all architected this way.

If our lives are shaped by narrative, then we must ask what

role the sacred narratives of our Scriptures—the Bible—play in molding and contouring our existence. Like all good stories, the place to begin, of course, is at the beginning.

Hearing the Story Again for the First Time

Let's adopt for a moment the mind-set of a writer from a couple of thousand years BC. I hate to be iconoclastic, but I don't think the author of Genesis was trying to give us an encyclopedic guide into which we can fit dinosaurs, calculate dates, count up generations, and devise scientifically plausible answers to our modern questions such as, "How old is the earth?" This is a creation *narrative*. It is a story. And let me be clear: "Story" isn't a category that requires something to be fiction. Calling Genesis "story" isn't a comment about it being fact or fiction. What I want to get past is forcing the Genesis author to answer twentieth-century questions on creation and evolution, for instance, when they weren't even remote categories in his thinking. He wasn't giving a blow-by-blow analysis that satisfies our scientific classrooms. Why? Because it wasn't the writer's goal; in fact, those questions didn't even exist. So let's return to the Genesis 1 narrative with storytellers' eyes and with story listeners' ears.

In the opening lines of Genesis, we find God speaking things into existence. He is shown to be the source of all that exists. In his speaking, he is doing something besides creating, though. He is shaping the created order into categories. The biblical text calls this "separating." His speaking has generative force and creative output—and his speaking separates. Think of these categories: light from darkness, day from night, evening from morning, "an expanse" to separate water from water, water from dry ground, and then a variety of separations in the plants and animals into groupings of various sorts. The summary refrain from all this generative speaking and creative separating and naming is they are all called "good."

We must not miss something that is often overlooked: God has the ability through his speaking to do this separating work, and it is called *good*. God's wholeness, his completeness, his integrity, in the truest sense of the word, isn't jeopardized as he splits things into groups. As he judges one thing from another and puts one thing in one category and another thing in another category, it is all *good*, according to the author. I don't want to belabor this, but we must highlight it because the fact that this refrain is mentioned over and over is a huge part of the *story*. Even in God's separating and naming function, there was still an unbroken unity of good underlying it all.

The recurring pronouncement in Genesis 1 that "it was good" is a clear statement that an alternative pronouncement "it was bad," or "it was evil," must have been possible. God's discernment or judging between things is good—not problematic, not driven by ego. It is done as a core reflection of what and who God is and of what is being done in the very creative act:

> Then God said, "Let us make human beings in our image, in our likeness, so that they may rule over the fish in the sea and the birds in the sky, over the livestock and all the wild animals, and over all the creatures that move along the ground."
>
> So God created human beings in his own image,
>   in the image of God he created them;
>   male and female he created them.
>
> God blessed them and said to them, "Be fruitful and increase in number; fill the earth and subdue it. Rule over the

fish in the sea and the birds in the sky and over every living creature that moves on the ground."

Genesis 1:26–28

Something unique happens in this part of the story. God marks man and woman as different from all other living creatures. This is made clear by two statements. Man and woman are made *imago dei*, in the image of God, and they are given the authority to rule over the rest of creation. They have been bestowed with uniqueness.

What if our starting point in talking to people about God, spiritual things, and Jesus—who he is and what he did—was the common ground that everyone acknowledges and senses: "You have been made in the image of God"? In some way, shape, or form, there is a God-like something inside each human being. I wonder what would happen if that became a new starting point for a new conversation.

Transfer of Power

The phrase in Genesis 1:26 "Let us" has perplexed and aroused the interest of scholars for a long time. Many of us have been taught that this is some sort of cryptic self-reference made by the Trinity. Some scholars, however, are quite convinced this is an image of the royal court, where God as King is making conversation and proclaiming something to those in his court.[1] A similar court scene is found in the opening chapters of Job.

The royal court observation is important for our conversation and for our understanding of the story of this first chapter of Genesis. For years, scholars and pastors have debated about what it means that we are made in the image of God. Various interpretations have been offered.[2] But most compelling to the biblical and cultural context is the fact that Adam and Eve were given the opportunity to benevolently and creatively serve/rule the world, the birds in the sky, and the fish in the sea.

Two different times in the three verses cited above—the end of verse 26 and end of verse 28—Adam and Eve were given a mandate: "rule." Given the royal court context of this story, this mandate is noteworthy to the careful reader. God delivers to human beings the creative and benevolent serving/rulership that he has apparently been doing himself with his royal court. If God, in his royal court, is doing the speaking, creating, naming, and ruling, why would God and the royal court punt that responsibility to mere creatures?

Is it possible that this transfer of royal rule is, at least in part, what it means to be made in the image of God? What if this spiritual DNA of ruling, serving, naming, and creating is part of the transformational architecture at the core of all of humans? What if the kernel, the seed of our deepest quests, is captured in this piece of 'god' he has put into us from the beginning of creation? How ingenious is that? God's design and blueprint was to place at our core a piece of himself! The very architecture of our spirits cries out for transformation, for serving, for being a part of something world-sized.

What we think happened at the fall has major implications for why we think Jesus even came to this earth. I again want to suggest we have inherited and then parroted a rather milquetoast and watered-down version of the story of the creation narrative, and as a result it translates into a "tough to sell" story as to why Jesus came.

The deepest transformational motivations of the human heart are architected into this *imago dei* with which everyone has been created. And this should become a new starting point for spiritual conversations.

Three-Dimensional Living "Statues"

The Hebrew words used in Genesis 1:26 for "image" and "likeness" are important to this conversation. Our understanding will help us see more clearly what God set out to accomplish in the creation of humanity. I will spare you the Hebrew lesson and make this as painless as possible. The words in their simplest form usually stand for a three-dimensional statue or idol or raised wall relief, as on an ancient tablet. According to J. Richard Middleton, "a virtual consensus has been building since the beginning of the twentieth century among Old Testament scholars concerning the meaning of *imago dei* in Genesis."[3] The God who presides over creation, and who creatively serves and rules the world, creates a humanity with the same role. They are to represent God by creatively and lovingly serving the rest of the world.[4]

God's placement of his image in humanity stands as revolutionary because it challenges creation stories from other ancient Near Eastern and Mesopotamian cultures.[5] In these stories that also chronicle the birth of creation and humanity, several items stand out as massive divergences from the Bible's creation account and are therefore significant for our understanding.[6] When a king took over land or established a claim on new territory and people, he would erect a statue in his *image* and *likeness* as a reminder of who was in charge and who the people were to serve. In these creation stories, humans exist to serve the gods, meet the divine needs, and relieve the gods of their burdens.[7] In short, all other creation accounts see the role of humans as slaves.

In our creation account, God doesn't erect a statue of his image that we are to bow down to and worship as a reminder of who is in charge. The potent irony is that God forbids the making of any image that could depict him.[8] And instead of erecting an image or representation of himself, he essentially says, "My three-dimensional statue is human—alive; my image and likeness are built into the very pinnacle of all created things—humans."[9]

Furthermore, God does not create humans as slaves or servants to meet his needs. Noticeably absent from the Genesis narrative is any hint that the purpose of Adam and Eve is to somehow serve the Creator and relieve the royal court of their burdens; even the idea of worshiping the Creator is markedly absent. On the contrary, God created humanity for the purpose of benevolent, creative serving of the whole of creation. In other word, God creates cocreators. The speaking, separating, and naming function God demonstrates in the opening chapter of Genesis is in fact the very same speaking, separating, and naming function he gives to Adam in his first role as cocreator, when he tells Adam to name the animals.[10]

Nothing in this creation story indicates "the gods" were creating humans to serve them. This creation story is about God sharing himself with his creation through his created image bearers. Let's return for a moment to our earlier conversations about a metanarrative and power. Far from a narrative about an overarching power play, the Bible's creation account is a story of compassion, sharing, loving, and serving.

Also noticeably absent in the opening chapter of Genesis is the mandate to rule over each other. All of humanity, in all its maleness and femaleness—the complete image of God—is to rule over and serve the rest of the created order. The assumption and the model of Genesis 1 is that of creative artistry, benevolent service, loving rule over the rest of the created order. Middleton observes,

"Humans in God's image, I suggest, are expected to imitate this primal generosity in their own shared rule of the earth."[11]

Middleton further notes that this call to a generous rule stands in complete opposition to the creation stories of ancient Mesopotamia. In other nonbiblical creation accounts, humans are largely given the role of repetition and servitude. In the Akkadian and Sumerian myths, the gods are the ones who act in history and change the course of human affairs. In some cases, the kings and priests can represent the gods and act on their behalf. But for *all humans* to be given the role of priest over creation, direction setter, designer, and artisan—this stands as unique.[12] The author points to the building of the Genesis 4:17 city and the engineering and design of the Genesis 11 tower, both of which illustrate the artistry and cocreative ability given humans made *imago dei*.

Can you see how all of the opening stories in the Genesis narrative invite us to view God, our world, and our lives in entirely different ways? These stories urge us to live into a narrative of how the world is and is meant to be—a very different approach from reading a narrative as a repository of truths to be mined and then applied. We can read these stories in such a way that we enter a *mythos* infusing us with hope, an understanding of self in relationship to God, and a world-sized vision of why we were created. This is far more compelling than our typical *logos* approaches that see the story as something to tear apart as we look for the universal truths that function as the keys to successful living.

Skyler Tactics and Philosophy

Chad and I had a standing golf date, which always proved to be great downtime from the office, great golf (well, most of the time), and stimulating conversation.

"Hey, man," I said as I walked up to join him. "What is this? I haven't even had time to hit a couple balls, and you're already on the first tee box ready to hit?"

Chad smiled. "Well, you were the one who told me this is how you got an edge with Skyler, so I thought I'd give it a try."

My son, Skyler, was an avid high school varsity golfer, and the previous summer was the first time I had experienced more check marks in the L column than in the W column. So whenever I got the chance, I would be on the first tee box waiting for Skyler to show up to play. He was already beating me most of the time, so I surely wasn't going to give him the benefit of warming up. This, of course, became quite the joke with Skyler and me, and now my sharing it with Chad was coming home to roost.

I began to slowly stretch out the kinks from sitting at my computer for the last couple of hours. Before I got much further, Chad said, "I have the topic for this eighteen-hole discussion." Chad and I had a conversation rhythm; at times I would set the stage for the conversation and pick Chad's brain, and at other times he would come with the topic or some questions and want to dialogue. Today was apparently one of those Chad-sets-the-tempo days.

"OK, man, take your shot. I mean that literally and verbally—hit the ball and then tell me the topic."

Chad banged one out, and then without waiting for the ball to drop, he said, "What is this 1P, 2P, 3P understanding of God thing I've heard and read about?"[13] His ball dropped at the edge of the rough, but he kept on talking. "On a website the other night I watched a video clip of a philosopher talking to some Benedictine monk about how Christianity in the West is totally geared to understanding God from a 2P, or second person perspective, and that there are two other dimensions, which many faith traditions entirely embrace but which Protestant Christianity struggles to come to grips with. Thoughts?"

"Yeah, I have some thoughts; but my thoughts at the moment are hitting my first shot—and since you haven't let me warm up and you've decided to do your little brain dump before I even get to hit, I'm thinking you want to win real bad today. So if you could just hit pause, Chad, and watch my swing of beauty, I would really appreciate it."

He chuckled. I whacked one.

The day was spectacular. Bright blue sky, perfectly manicured grass, and brilliant green, mature trees just coming into their fullness after a rainy spring. There was brand-new white sand in all the sand traps, making them stick out on the golfscape like mouths begging for little white round morsels to eat.

As we started down the first fairway, I picked up on his conversation starter. "Well, believe it or not, this is a topic I've spent some time thinking about. Our understanding of God in the Western tradition has been dominated by an—"

"An I-Thou understanding," Chad said. "They were talking about that last night and quoted the Jewish philosopher Martin Buber, whom I've read."

"What haven't you read, Chad? You are killing me, man. I can hardly keep up with you, and this is supposed to be my area. But yes, you are right. We have understood God almost exclusively in "God is out there as a person somewhere" categories—and when that story doesn't connect with people, they are pretty much out of luck." I reached into the top pocket of my golf bag to grab some gum and asked Chad if he was chewing. He nodded and stared at me, waiting for me to continue. "Listen, I'm not making excuses here, but so much of our Christianity has been about protecting the way we already understand it, about making sure the interpretations we have never change. So it's hard for us to think about some of these issues in fresh ways. You grew up in the church; I'm sure you understand that."

He took his second shot and dropped his ball on the edge of the green.

"I hate to admit it," I said after my ball found the sand, "but I realize that a good deal of Christian ministry is about making sure people have the right interpretation of things. The 'right interpretation' is usually what their denomination says, or what some era—for example, the Reformation—has said, or what some pastor has said. Unfortunately, a lot of these interpretations are adopted wholesale without examination, and we roll along on our merry way, rarely asking hard questions about the inherited ideas and positions."

Chad nodded his head vigorously. "This is one of the things I don't get about Christianity. Isn't there a realization that we need careful thinking about how to tell people about Christianity in a post-9/11 world? So many people I know think God must be powerless to deal with things such as terrorism or tsunamis or slave trafficking or blood diamonds—because if God weren't powerless, then wouldn't he do something?"

I exhaled firmly through pursed lips, letting him hear my angst about this issue. "You are bringing up the thorny and difficult 'problem of evil,' as it has been traditionally called."

"But it runs at a more personal level for me," said Chad. "I'm not so interested in the philosophical or theological answer to this. My problem is ultrapractical. I recognize that, try as I might, I can't get out of my head that God is out there, watching over us like a taskmaster to make sure we don't get out of line." He paused and looked at me and said, "Gap or lob wedge." I whispered, "Gap," and he continued. "I'm not trying to be dramatic or simplistic, but here's the dilemma: Deep down I have trouble shaking the image of God as judge when all the while the Christian message is that *God is love*."

"At least that's supposed to be the message," I muttered.

Chad nodded and went on. "All these events in our world just seem to affirm the 'God is out there being a judge' view. The whole idea that we've all committed some major infraction and that unless we go to hell to pay for it, or have someone else pay for it—like Jesus—then we are doomed. How is that a God of either love or justice?"

"Wow, do I resonate, Chad! I grew up in a Catholic and Presbyterian home—and you know what? Deep down, I have that same view of God—that God isn't primarily love—and I've been struggling with it my whole life." I walked over to the little weatherproof box containing scorecards placed there strategically for those too rushed at the first tee box to remember to get one from the clubhouse. I looked at my cohort in crime and asked, "Are we keeping score?" He tilted his head and rolled his eyes. The answer was essentially, "Heck, yes, are you kidding me?"

I continued on along the same vein. "And we're not the only ones. I recently attended a conference where this very topic was discussed. And guess what? Out of the several hundred people present, almost everyone acknowledged that the 'God as judge ready to crack them' view was their primary view."

The conversation moved forward in a rush. Chad was really connecting the dots and had some great insights. This was a conversation with huge implications.

I want to echo something in this conversation with Chad that I have since tested on hundreds of churched people, many of whom were pastors. Chad's statement that he can't shake the image of God as judge is a common problem, and I think this may be one of the biggest problems we will have to overcome as we enter spiritual conversations.

I have asked people at conferences and in churches to get in touch with the dominant and reflexive understanding of God that comes to mind when the word *God* is used. I then give them the two options: *God is love and wants to care, nurture, and support you*—or *God is a judge watching to make sure you obey and do the right thing.* At least 75 percent of the people I ask acknowledge that their dominant and reflexive understanding of God is that he is the judge. In some settings, almost the entire audience sees God as judge.

If those of us inside the Christian church, those who have spent their whole lives reading the Bible and learning about the God who in 1 John 4:7–8 is defined as love, can't shake the image of God as judge, do you think those outside the church have a better view? Wouldn't it make sense that their reflexive thought about God would also be that he is the judge? I suspect that if you were to do your own informal surveying, you would find that most people's dominant understanding of God is as "Other," as "God out there somewhere," as second person. This was the theme Chad was picking up on.

If those outside the faith see God as a judge ready to crack us when we get out of line, what would entice them to explore Christianity? And when you take into consideration the church's reluctance to transform its notions about God from judge to lover, we don't have a very compelling offer to make. My sense is that most churches live out of the consciousness that God is judge by adopting the mind-set that they, too, are judges acting on behalf of God. It is precisely this judgmentalism that convinces those outside the church to look elsewhere for a message of wholeness and shalom.

Spiritual Surgery

Janna couldn't have been more different from Mandisa, the woman I had met in South Africa. Janna was a white, middle-class college freshman from the western United States. But her response couldn't have been more similar when it came to "aha" moments about *imago dei*.

"Ron, understanding this thing about *imago dei* just caused something to break in me. I haven't been able to hold back the tears since you started talking about it. I've gone to church my whole life, but I've never heard about *imago dei*. I know I'm a sinner. I grew up hearing it most Sundays, and the life I lived in the sorority would give plenty of evidence to support that premise. But I've lived an empty life. I have everything, but nothing is satisfying. I've been told I need Jesus, and I have Jesus. But hearing that I'm made in the image of the very God of the universe? Something happened in me. I can't even describe it. It feels like major surgery deep in my spirit, and I just sobbed most of the night as you talked. Something is being healed, or maybe I'm being converted all over again. I am *imago dei*, and that reality has changed me tonight."

CHAPTER 5

You and Me — Gods?

"This is what has been missing. I get it! This makes total sense to me. Why didn't someone just say this?" Jake was a high schooler letting out a barrage of thoughts. He was in the student ministries of one of the churches I had been working with for a couple years and known as teetering between agnostic and atheist. A very intelligent kid and something of an autodidact on topics of philosophy and religion, Jake had attended a couple of the evening classes I taught, even though they were set up for adults. A number of young people who had questions about the Bible had started to attend. Though we hadn't had any interaction until the previous month's session, when he had stuck around to ask some questions, this particular night was different.

"Tonight was really helpful in putting some stuff into my conversation bank that I can think about. Every religious tradition I've studied has some measure of 'humans have a divine center' at the core of their philosophy. It just never made sense to me that Christianity was negative from the beginning when everyone else seemed to start positive."

Jake said this with the smugness that only a self-studied eighteen-year-old high schooler could get away with. Having twenty-one- and eighteen-year-old sons of my own made this an easy connection and caused a grin to spread on my face. "So the big takeaway tonight is what, Jake?" I prodded him to continue with his flurry of insights.

"If we are little gods, so to speak—if we are the ones called to carry on the look and feel and flavor of God in this world—then that's a pretty cool place for the story to begin. That means the point of the whole story is quite different. Now it isn't about fixing something that's screwed up; it's about fulfilling God's original reason for creating us and the world in the first place. OK, that's something worth chewing on. See you next month, Ron. Thanks for the food for thought. And you know what? This *imago dei* thing might make a great tat!"

Imago Dei Design Features

I want to lay out a possibility: What if the *imago dei* in all of us is placed there as God's divinely designed architecture of our spirit? What if this architecture is a sort of compass that drives people to explore, gravitate toward, and be interested in spiritual things and the ultimate transformation they can bring? What if our job is simply to help people realize where the compass is pointing them?

What is so big about this little Genesis 1 foray into *imago dei*? I wonder if it may be pointing us toward starting the spiritual conversation at an entirely different place. God's story starts with his crowning humanity as a coruler, cocreator, creative artisan with him. Paul uses similar language in the New Testament.[1] Our storying of a God out there who is about to banish us to an eternal torture chamber unless we buy into a certain set of propositions is simply not connecting. The postmodern psyche doesn't have the sense of "the Other"—the transcendent God—that previous generations had. The primary fall-redemption narrative, which is about guilt alleviation of the heinous crimes and infinitely offensive infractions I have committed against the Other, is not a story, correct or not, that will communicate in our culture.[2]

The second person (2P) way of understanding God is clearly part of the Christian perspective and doesn't need to be challenged. This 2P concept, however, is clearly not connecting in our culture. I suggest we have available in our Christian repertoire more theological material we can bring to the conversation table. Can we eventually get to the second person discussion but start with the interests and drives people already seem to have? Apparently a significant number of people have no interest in the idea of pursuing God "out there," as second person. But why, then, all the spiritual interest? What is all this interest about if it isn't about the 2P God, the God who is a person "out there"?

Inward Journey

Our culture has already hinted that it is having *imago dei* conversations; it just doesn't call them by that name. While American culture is substantially deaf to conversations concerning the second person (2P) rendition of God, where he is viewed as "Other," we *are* having conversations in bars, coffee shops, study groups, golf courses (for Chad and me) about the "god within"—a first person (1P) understanding of God. They aren't particularly interested in the God out there because that God is often presented by the church as a judgmental taskmaster who is really a bit egotistical and has "issues." But they are extremely interested in spiritual things—and even in God. The "God out there" method has been presented and found wanting; maybe another approach—"finding God within"—will get better mileage.

The outward versus inward journey describes one of the big differences between the Eastern and Western traditions of Christianity. At the risk of oversimplifying, in the West, the journey toward God is a journey outward to the Other; in the East, the journey toward God is an inward journey to the quiet place where God has placed his image and spirit.

It is obvious to me that many of us—whether evangelical, postevangelical, or recovering evangelical—will find this first person approach foreign. But just because it is foreign doesn't mean we need to reject it before exploring it. Tradition has been a perennial problem for those in the church who conclude, "If it sounds unfamiliar, it is suspect." Anything suspect doesn't warrant much investigation, except with skeptical eyes. Investigation tinged with skepticism doesn't allow us to suspend judgment long enough to really hear. Without suspending judgment, we listen from a spot that will only confirm our preconceived ideas and further entrench our thinking into the old exhausted paradigm.

A New Entry Point

A first person understanding of God is not the only new entry point needing further exploration. Huge numbers of people are increasingly concerned about the environment and the living, breathing organism of creation. Many people see God in nature. They see God's handiwork and have an innate sense that we are somehow responsible for taking care of this place. We might characterize this as a "God in creation."

This is a third person (3P), "it" view of God, if you will. Your individual posture toward the environment is secondary. Adam's quite literal physical connection to the dirt (*adamah* in Hebrew) and his and Eve's mandate to take care of the earth should be enough for us to recognize that people are hovering over material we should be willing to have God-conversations about.

Much needs to be explored here, and I hope, by pointing out that a fuller view of God has all three of these dimension, we can have more constructive, progressive conversations about 1P and 3P perspectives. What if we began to develop excellent resources and to ask questions that would engage people at the 1P and 3P levels? What if, instead of fear and control being our reflexive responses to these ideas, we were able to suspend judgment and get in touch with resources already available in other strands of our Christian tradition? What if we refused to let new thoughts threaten us but rather allowed them to open us up to new possibilities? What if we were willing to hold with intellectual and spiritual humility our understandings and our certainty about the way we've always done things?

Let me be quick to state I'm not suggesting that the 1P or 3P view of God is complete or adequate. What I *am* suggesting is that when we start the conversation with a fall-redemption paradigm, we are talking about God only in second person, which isn't adequate either. A construal of the Christian story that starts at the fall is a misrepresentation of the story, and we ought to be glad that people are rejecting it. When we start with creation and Genesis 1, we instantly enter a world in which every person has been vested with the image of God, with God-like authority, qualities, and mandates. Everyone finds resonance because there is an architecture built into us for these things.

Certainly some understandings of God in second person (2P) are legitimate. This is where we are most comfortable. Some understandings of God in first person (1P)—like *imago dei*—are also legitimate ideas we should pursue. No doubt God is in creation in some way (3P)—we can look to passages in Scripture such as the personification of creation in Psalm 19 (nature speaks) and Romans 8 (creation groans) that show we have resources at our disposal that would encourage these conversations.

Radiant Gods

In our Protestant church tradition, we don't have many categories for understanding this first person, God-within pursuit. One of the issues on which the Eastern and Western church significantly differ has to do with the very passages of Scripture where a first person view of God is possible.[3] Try to read these passages again, as if for the first time:

> "We are not stoning you for any good work," they replied, "but for blasphemy, because you, a mere man, claim to be God."
>
> Jesus answered them, "Is it not written in your Law, 'I have said you are "gods"'? If he called them 'gods,' to whom the word of God came—and Scripture cannot be broken—what about the one whom the Father set apart as his very own and sent into the world? Why then do you accuse me of blasphemy because I said, 'I am God's Son'?"
>
> John 10:33–36

> Don't you know that you yourselves are God's temple and that God's Spirit dwells in your midst? If anyone destroys God's temple, God will destroy that person; for God's temple is sacred, and you together are that temple.
>
> 1 Corinthians 3:16–17

Do you not know that your bodies are temples of the Holy Spirit, who is in you, whom you have received from God? You are not your own.

1 Corinthians 6:19

To them God has chosen to make known among the Gentiles the glorious riches of this mystery, which is Christ in you, the hope of glory.

Colossians 1:27

His divine power has given us everything we need for a godly life through our knowledge of him who called us by his own glory and goodness. Through these he has given us his very great and precious promises, so that through them you may participate in the divine nature, having escaped the corruption in the world caused by evil desires.

2 Peter 1:3–4

Dear friends, now we are children of God, and what we will be has not yet been made known. But we know that when Christ appears, we shall be like him, for we shall see him as he is.

1 John 3:2

This sort of "reading the Bible again for the first time" exercise requires significant humility and a willingness to realize we may not have it all figured out. I can't do full commentary on these passages at this point, but I will say that these passages are understood in Christian traditions other than evangelical Protestantism to mean that a journey inward toward God is just as legitimate as a journey outward toward God. Many of us in our tradition have no room for alternative readings, but perhaps this is one of the reasons we are at an impasse on the spiritual conversation front. I wonder if we are so concerned about protecting our prior readings of these passages that we can't hear any other options—options that may enhance our experience of knowing God.

Some of the passages quoted above would be tough to swallow if we couldn't see the truth in the 1P vision of God. Listen to what one of the most-quoted theologians of the previous generation writes about the John 10 passage. I quote him because of the vast respect he has garnered over the years, making him one of the great voices of the twentieth century:

> Morality is indispensable: but the Divine Life, which gives itself to us and which calls us to be gods, intends for us something in which morality will be swallowed up. We are to be re-made.... we shall find underneath it all a thing we have never yet imagined: a real Man, an ageless god, a son of God, strong, radiant, wise, beautiful, and drenched in joy.[4]

> [God] said (in the Bible) that we were "gods" and He is going to make good His words. If we let Him—for we can prevent Him, if we choose—He will make the feeblest and filthiest of us into a god or goddess, dazzling, radiant, immortal creature, pulsating all through with such energy and joy and wisdom and love as we cannot now imagine, a bright stainless mirror which reflects back to God perfectly (though, of course, on a smaller scale) His own boundless power and delight and goodness. The process will be long and in parts very painful; but that is what we are in for.[5]

Shocked at C. S. Lewis? Many people are when they realize that Lewis has a highly developed 1P perspective. I quote him to help us see that the idea of us being "little gods" (what is called *theosis* or divinization) isn't relegated to far-off monks in an Eastern Orthodox monastery in Siberia or in a Buddhist study center in the Himalayan foothills in Tibet.[6] It is a topic that finds outlet and expression in much of our Christian history—both ancient and modern.[7] I think we get worked up about *theosis* because in it we hear risky language. But when we recognize that God wants us to be little gods, then we begin to come to know God in new and fresh ways. The best way to safeguard ourselves is to recognize that, while we are called to be gods, our god-ness is always derivative and therefore diminutive. Note that Lewis was careful to keep the creature/Creator distinction. He wasn't interested in confusing the created human with the uncreated Creator. But neither was he timid about using the word *gods* for us as creatures.

Push-Backs to Push-Throughs

At a recent conference, a guy flagged me down after a session I did on the 1P, 2P, and 3P views of God. He asked, "Ron, do you think that entering into a 1P conversation is affirming a view of God that is incomplete and possibly incorrect? Don't you think we should just stick with the orthodox, tried-and-true approach?" We had a great conversation in the hallway, and I conceded that the 1P conversation *is* incomplete. But I also helped him push through the "orthodox, tried-and-true approach" that didn't seem to be getting the results we wanted. He admitted to being among those who raised their hands when I asked if their view of God was reflexively that of a judge. So as he leaned against the wall in the hallway, he began to see that his view of God was incomplete and needed further expansion. This was a great bridge into further conversation. I shared my struggle with the traditional altar call model common in many churches—judging exactly who was in and who wasn't and when someone had changed camps. He put his head down as he shook it from side to side. Without even responding to any questions from me, he acknowledged that counting the noses of those who had responded to an appeal was a huge motivator for him. He said something to the effect that it was the only scorecard he knew.

Many of us—even long-standing Christ-followers—have an inaccurate view of God as primarily a judge and have a hard time seeing God as love.[8] Inaccurate and incomplete understandings about God from the 1P perspective don't make 2P understandings automatically more accurate, complete, or orthodox. We need to radically rethink all three arenas—1P, 2P and 3P—and understand how they contribute to a fuller understanding of God. I would suggest that without all three understandings contributing to a full-orbed view of God, we will have a flattened story and will leave ourselves with severely limited resources for the conversation.

As long as Christianity is primarily understood as a batch of propositions in which God is judging how well we execute them, we will have problems getting people interested in the story, primarily because it is an uninteresting and inaccurate downer. But when we return to the story as drama—a drama in which we have been invited to play a crucial role—then we end up with a powerful interplay of Creator-God, Cocreator-Son, and the Divine Spirit energizing it all. The Cocreator-Son is where the human dimension enters the divine drama. As Jesus is the incarnation of God in the divine drama unfolding on the earth, we are the ongoing incarnation of Jesus on this earth in the ongoing unfolding drama.

The prolific theologian Hans Urs von Balthasar writes rich words in which we see the intersection of 1P and 2P understandings of God:

Christianity is not a teaching but an action that God undertakes, the playing out of the drama that God began with mankind in the Old Covenant. The key to understanding the action lies solely in God's presentation of himself to human beings on the stage of human nature, by virtue of the identity of the divine "Author," the divine and human "Actor," and the divine Spirit, who exists identically in both and who interprets the action for those whom the Actor has brought into the drama.[9]

The point here isn't which perspective on God is right and which is wrong—a polarity prominent in the modern world of education—or which view is more accurate or complete. My point for the purpose of spiritual conversations is *starting location.* Why don't we start spiritual conversations within the context and framework everyone understands, resonates with, and buys into without any persuasion?

Our typical approach of dismissing something that doesn't fit well within the confines of our well-worn readings is a tragedy when we realize that many of those tired and tattered readings are accepted without examination and adopted at an early stage in our faith development.

If our theological repertoire is deficient due to fear of overstatement—often the very fear that lurks in this discussion about humans being God—then we must do some careful thinking and dialoguing. Fear shouldn't set the parameters of the conversation. Lack of hard thinking and well-defined terms shouldn't short-circuit the resources available to us. An inability to control the outcome of these kinds of conversations shouldn't cause us to lapse into a rote, dead, *logos* religion. It certainly didn't stop C. S. Lewis from making some direct statements—statements that seem out-of-bounds to many evangelicals. And the power, the beauty, and the *mythos* of the statements he made? Wow!

■

"What a bridge this creates for me to use." Cindy was a full-time stay-at-home mom, who loved God's Word and loved sharing her faith. "Ron, this is the piece I really needed to help carry on conversation with the gals who are talking about the Oprah Winfrey–Eckhart Tolle webcast that was on several months ago. A bunch of my girlfriends invited me to do the book study with—and I sort of, well, I told them I couldn't. You know, it isn't biblical! It's hostile to the right path to following Jesus. At least that's what I was thinking when I politely declined. Now I see that their desire to study the book may simply show how deeply they want to engage spiritual things, and this 1P idea may help me understand things from a slightly different vantage point."

"Cindy, you don't need to be part of this book study to be able to carry on conversations with the gals, you know. You can talk with them guilt free, without feeling you have to quote Bible verses or bring biblical critique to every idea they raise."

"That is the million-dollar takeaway from tonight's class," Cindy responded. "I don't have to play 'theology policeman.' What I learned tonight is so liberating as I go out and try to carry on spiritual conversations that are much less hostile and charged."

CHAPTER 6

The Infectious Judger Gene

I was in the checkout lane, drumming my fingers on the candy rack and wishing that the lady in front of me would hurry up and pay her tab. Her kids were running around like they hadn't been out of the house in three months. What really irritated me was that she seemed oblivious to the fact that they were running into people, including me, smacking each other, yelling, knocking over candy boxes, and essentially making a scene. And boy oh boy, did my judger voice begin to say to myself, *Are you kidding me? Control your freakin' kids. I need to get you a parenting brochure. This is a public place, not an outdoor playground. Get some awareness, lady. These are your kids.*

Yeah, I know, not pretty thoughts from a supposed Christian, pastor, spiritual leader, huh? Pretty ugly, quite honestly. But something happened that proved to be a watershed in my own spiritual journey. As this frazzled mom paid for her items, she said to the cashier, "Thank you for being patient with me. This has been a hard week. I'm taking care of my dying mother at my house, and my husband left me this week."

I was bowled over by a nauseous wave of "You big idiot, Ron."

In that moment, a couple of insights hit me that I have never forgotten: I realized how entrenched judging is inside of me. And I realized how quickly I jump to conclusions without taking into account what might be a host of reasons and rationales for a person's behavior. Replaying that scene is a vivid reminder that I need to let the judger in me die.

Selfless to Selfish: The Grand Shift

The grand shift from being benevolent, loving, caring stewards to malevolent, selfish, self-absorbed rulers shows the dominant infection we all have. Further, this shift from selfless to selfish is the engine behind wanting to judge who is in and who is out. Not coincidentally, the one doing the judging is always in.

I've been a part of a learning community for several years now. Vortex Learning Community, now called Spiritual Explorations Live, is a group of about thirty to forty people who get together for extended conversation on everything from string theory and the origins of the universe to current books being written on spirituality to philosophy and biblical theology.[1] No sermons, no actual teaching, but Socratic questioning around topics we have read and then engaging in dialogue. We keep the dialogue going through the week on a chat board until we reconvene in real life. One of our goals was to create a judgment-free zone where we could discuss any topic without someone instantly correcting us or shooting down our ideas. We were learning the art of genuine dialogue—learning to suspend judgment and come to shared meanings. One of the women in our learning community shared a perceptive and insightful reflection on the Genesis narrative in one conversation. She said, "I am coming more and more to see sin as the illusion of my separateness." Eve's and Adam's eating of the fruit was prompted by the illusion that they were independent and had no connection or responsibility to anything else.

The background for the word *sin* comes out of the world of archery, pointing to sin as "missing the mark or target." Most of the time when we miss the mark, we are functioning as though our decisions and actions are independent and unconnected. In the truest sense of the word, this is what *egocentric* means: I (*ego* in Greek) am at the center. Everything flows from or connects to the center hub—namely, me! This definition applies to how we interact not only with each other but with God and the creation around us as well. We have been infected with the illusion that we live independent, separate, and sovereign lives. Again, this infection of separateness is not simply an exercise in theological reflection; it strikes to the heart of why Jesus came, why we think people need Jesus. If we can understand this issue better, I think we will be able to find a better entrance point for our spiritual conversations about Jesus.

Architecture Fissures from Infections

Enter Mr. Serpent into the story. Adam and Eve decided the temptation to become like God was too great.[2] In eating the fruit from this tree, they would have the ability to know good from evil—and they just couldn't stop themselves.

God's creative ability was expressed not only in what was created but also in God's ability to separate things and make pronouncements of what is good and what is not good. Were Adam and Eve tempted by the idea that if they ate the fruit they would have the separating ability of God—something they already shared with God in part by naming and separating the animals into groups? Or were they tempted by eating from the forbidden tree so that in addition to naming and separating they would also have the ability to know whether something was good or evil? It appears from the text that they would acquire the ability to make pronouncements that only God, with his perfect and infinite knowledge, would be able to make. They would presumably be seeking to make the sort of pronouncements that God had made in the refrain of Genesis, namely, "and it was good."

Could a human being, a created being, ever have the ability to really know the absolute difference between good and evil? Could a finite being ever handle knowledge of that magnitude? The answer is apparently no. Isn't the knowledge of good and evil a perspective that would be exclusively the domain of an all-knowing God. We aren't told specifically why God put this particular tree off-limits. We do know exactly what happens once they eat its fruit, though.

Primary Symptom

Once Adam and Eve eat from the tree of the knowledge of good and evil, the result is instantaneous. They immediately begin to judge between good and evil. And yet the results of their judging seem to be significantly different from God's appraisal. This is a notable piece of the story we shouldn't gloss over too quickly.

Adam and Eve instantly notice their physical differences. Their judgment of those differences was that they were evil for the naked eye to behold (pun intended). They remedy their nakedness by covering their individual distinctiveness. Judging their distinctiveness is something related to their fruit eating, because one of the things God asks them when they are hiding from him is how they know they are naked. Part of the infection Adam and Eve contract is a desire to judge, which is just another way of talking about an ability to "know good and evil."

Their ability to know good from evil, though, can never be realized in any ultimate way. All of Adam and Eve's knowledge is from a limited human perspective. So this particular area having to do with good and evil will surely be no different. Their knowing what is truly good and truly evil is simply impossible without the limitless knowledge and perspective of God. This is apparently one of those definite distinctions between the Creator and the created. And even though they are made in the image of God, they are not the same, in terms of knowledge, as the limitless Creator-God who brought them into being. Omniscience is one of the classical attributes of God that defines God as God—a characteristic Adam and Eve do not share.

Symptom Severity

Part of the sickness introduced by Adam and Eve is our incessant desire to judge between good and not good (evil), even though we are incapable of doing so in any ultimate sort of way. If we start with the Cain and Abel story and move on into the New Testament, one of the recurring problems within the human condition is the desire and drive to judge, to make distinctions, to make our own pronouncements—even as the ability to do so is vastly limited. One of the reasons we are limited is simply because we aren't God, and so we don't have the full perspective. We aren't all-knowing. This partial knowledge—what the apostle Paul called, "seeing through a glass, darkly"[3]—is one of the very things that often gets us in trouble.

One of the biggest issues the church faces when it comes to spiritual conversations is judgment. I would suggest all of our judging of who is in and who is out, of who is acceptable and who is not, of who is God's and who is not—all of those judgments between good and evil—can be traced all the way back to the foundational temptation faced by Adam and Eve. Furthermore, these are the very things Jesus challenged the religious establishment to stop doing. Over and over we see Jesus warn against judging and against drawing lines to determine who is in and out.[4]

The Gospels are full of stories where the religious leaders of the day were bound and determined to draw lines so that tax collectors were out, to recite laws so that disciples plucking grain on the Sabbath were out, to highlight Sabbath-keeping regulations so that Jesus' healing on the Sabbath was out, and to talk about hand-washing rituals so that Jesus' disciples were out.

Jesus' story in Matthew 13 about the weeds and the wheat is essentially about forbidding the disciples to pull up weeds because pulling weeds is a call only God can make. Only God has the knowledge that ensures that when a weed is pulled, wheat isn't uprooted along with it. Read Jesus' explanation of this story a little later in the narrative. Clearly it is not up to humans to do the ultimate judging.

These stories and many others point to the deep human drive to draw lines about who is in and who is out, to judge, to sit in positions of superiority over other humans. And where did it all begin? Adam and Eve—with the first illustration being their son Cain, who judged that his brother, Abel, deserved death because God preferred Abel's offering to his (see Genesis 4). Jesus went to great lengths to transcend divisive boundaries and instead to include and invite. Much more could be said, but the point is clear: Part of the infection passed on from Adam and Eve—and directly related to their eating from the tree of the knowledge of good and evil—is an obsession to judge without the perfect knowledge to do so. We are unable as creatures to do the work that is reserved for the Creator. God passed on to Adam and Eve as *imago dei* many things, but one thing clearly absent was any statement that they were to judge between good and evil.

One of the very actions related to the story of the fall in Genesis—and challenged by Jesus throughout his ministry—is one of the primary things the church is known for, namely, judging.[5] The primary organism called to accept people as is, with the love of God and open arms, is known throughout the land as one of the most caustic, legalistic, moralistic, and judgmental places on the planet. This breaks my heart, as I'm sure it does yours. I love the local church. I believe that God is at work in and through the local church. The bummer, of course, is that there are so many churches that have judgmentalism in their blind spot. And what you can't see, you can't acknowledge and change. We must become more self-evaluative and open to criticism and dialogue from within.

Can you see how understanding the infection of Adam and Eve helps us understand not only why Jesus came but also how that infection has become one of the primary deterrents to spiritual conversations about God and Jesus in our time? Jesus accepted prostitutes without judgment. He had dinner with the rip-off artists known as tax collectors. He was willing to hang with and be seen with those everyone else within "the church" had already judged as "out." He made it clear it was the sick who needed a doctor.[6] He came to bring wholeness to the broken, no matter what form that brokenness took. I've had to realize that until I can let the judger in me die, I am greatly jeopardizing my voice in my task of carrying on authentic spiritual conversations about Jesus, who was willing to include all sorts of people who had been judged as "out."

In the midst of not judging the woman caught in adultery, is it surprising that Jesus didn't get into a conversation with her about her eternal destiny, about whether or not she was going to repent or was sorry for the lifestyle she was living? Jesus never had any such conversation, though he did tell her to leave her life of sin.[7] Shouldn't that give us pause as to what the main message of Jesus was?

As we return to considering the Adam and Eve story, another irony emerges. If our understanding of *imago dei* is correct, Adam and Eve had been made in God's image and likeness and as such were *already* like God; yet the serpent told them they would be like God if they ate from the tree in the middle of the garden. Not only did they disobey God; they sought something they already possessed at some level. They *were* like God — made in God's image and likeness — though they were not given ultimate power or ultimate knowledge like that of the Creator. They were as much like God as they could have been without *being* God.

It is important to note, however, that the author of Genesis restates that human beings are made in the image of God — the *imago dei* is still intact and being passed on to subsequent generations, even though the infection resulting from the fall has deadly consequences.[8] I think the author of Genesis wants to make sure we realize that while there is an infection, it has not displaced God's design and architecture. Those yearnings and longings are still there; they are just bent now — altered and tinged but not displaced or replaced.

Chad on Spiritual Genetics

Chad and I were teeing off on the eighteenth hole and ready to call it a night. We had been having a great conversation all evening about Adam and Eve being tempted with and then infected by the "judger gene."

"That is one of the more nuanced understandings of the Genesis 1 account I've heard," Chad said as he put the head cover back on his driver. "You know, Ron, I think the issue of judging may be one of the biggest marketing nightmares the church faces, because for all the things the church is not good at, she seems to be expert at judging people."

I couldn't have agreed more with Chad, but I wanted to hear him unpack that thought. "What do you think is going on with all the judging?"

The sun was heading down behind the pines on the left side of the fairway, and you could see it puncturing the fence around the tennis courts in the distance. Chad pulled out his 3-wood and prepared to take a shot. "I think we have this judger inside us that just longs for an outlet," he said. "I guess that is what you are saying the Christian story says. We constantly struggle with this bone marrow-deep infection. I see this in my life, and I certainly see it in most people's lives. In fact, I'd be willing to bet that most people, or at least most people I know, would agree we often exhibit an essentially 'look out for number one' streak."

He hit a great second shot, which landed right in front of the green. I was a bit jealous and told him that apparently all this philosophical talk wasn't hurting his game at all.

He tossed me a cocky grin but stayed on topic. "Here's my question: Isn't a relationship with Jesus supposed to help reverse the trend? Fix the infection? Quiet the judger? Reacquaint us with compassion so we reverse the effects of judging? This is where it seems to me everything breaks down terribly."

Chad knew there were parts of his theory I bought and other things I had concerns about.

"That is what we all hope will happen, but somehow Christianity hasn't always made people more compassionate and less judging; sometimes it makes us even more judging and less com-passionate," I said.

Chad eyeballed me as I took my shot, but began talking be-fore the ball even landed. "I realize you can't blame the founder for how the followers behave, but if Christians really think that following Jesus is so life transforming, shouldn't we expect to see transformation in the very areas that are most difficult and central to the infection?"

My approach shot to the green fell short of Chad's, but we were both lying two on this par 5 and getting ready to chip onto the green. "Before I respond, please allow the gallery to go silent while I pull a beautiful lob wedge shot out of my bag. Quiet please." It was a good shot onto the green, fifteen feet from the pin, but probably not birdie territory for my putting. I turned to Chad. "I do think we should see transformation, but we don't always see it in compelling, serious ways. And certainly not to the magnitude that the dominant characterization of Christianity is that of loving, accepting, and nonjudgmentally helping people find their way to God."

Chad chipped up to about the same distance from the pin, and we walked up and put our bags on the side of the green and pulled out our putters. "I think one of the most compelling things we've talked about today is this idea that Adam and Eve were given a sort of joint ownership with God and charged with some open-ended management responsibilities," Chad said. "I know that isn't what you called it, but it seems to me that's what it is. I think the definition the gal used in your learning community for sin as the 'illusion of separateness' is just brilliant. She has a great insight there."

Chad had hit a real spinner and left a major ball mark that he bent over to repair as I walked behind my ball to see what kind of work I had left to do.

"You know, most of my bad management calls are due to selfishness," Chad said. "I feel a need to keep my nose clean or to look better than maybe I really am. In almost every case, I'm living under the illusion of being separate from others I work with—the executive VP I report to and the peers I find myself so often manipulating. In each of these cases, I'm acting under the illusion that I'm separate from them. But I'm not."

"Chad, you need to be careful, buddy," I said, grinning. "I smell a full-blown change of heart and mind."

He grinned and shook his head no. "That won't be happening any time soon."

I looked him right in the eyes and told him, "I think it's already happening."

We both putted out, having missed our birdies but being content with pars. We headed over to the clubhouse to get a drink and finish our conversation.

As Chad scuffed the bottom of his golf shoe through the shoe brush outside the clubhouse door, he said, "Ron, that *is* the problem. We are *not* separate—not from God, not from each other, not from the environment. Our decisions have a ripple effect that we rarely take into consideration."

We walked in and found an empty table.

He looked at me and asked what the smirk was for. I just shook my head and said, "Chad, conversation at this level is so deeply satisfying because the stakes are so important."

He waved to the waitress and then turned back to me. "Well, I'm glad you like it so much because I want to keep talking a bit before we head home." We each ordered one of their amazing hot dogs, and then Chad continued. "Don't you think if we seriously thought we were all intimately related, we would treat each other differently? I mean, the way I look at it, I treat people in my family with a different sort of deference and respect than I do someone I run into at Wal-Mart."

"Sure. Family has a place of privilege."

Chad nodded. "On one hand that makes total sense, and yet on the other hand it violates the very thing we were just talking about—the fact that we are *all* deeply connected. We are not separate from each other."

The dogs arrived, and the waitress was balancing plates, condiments, and baskets of fries. We paused while she dump-trucked the whole load onto the table. "We had almost this exact discussion in our learning community the other night. I'm pretty sure it was this very discussion that brought on the idea about sin being the illusion of separateness. A couple of the people in our community were reading a book called *No Boundaries*.[9] The essential idea is this one you've just raised."

"You mean the idea of treating family differently from a department store stranger?" Chad asked.

"Yeah, we make these artificial concentric circles where we place closest to us those who are most like us—and therefore of course more acceptable, lovable, easy to get along with. You get the idea."

Chad picked up the thought. "So family is on the inner circle, kind of the 'friends and family plan' of the cell phone commercials, huh? Friends a little further out, strangers further out still."

"That's right," I said. "And it doesn't stop there. We do the same thing with other living creatures, creation, and even inanimate objects."

Chad looked up after grabbing a handful of fries and said, "I totally do that. That which is most like me is closest to the center and gets treated accordingly, and those further out are also treated accordingly. Wow! Very insightful."

"This is what someone said in the midst of the conversation the other night. Isn't the making of these boundary circles part of the infection? Isn't this what Adam and Eve did in identifying their individual differences? Isn't this the beginning of what appears to be innocuous judging?"

Chad was nodding his head, tracking with me the whole way. He asked, "Isn't this exactly what Jesus was trying to get the Pharisees to see, that the boundaries they had erected were false and destructive and ultimately prevented them from being able to love their neighbors?"

"You have a good memory, even though you've been away from church for a long time," I told him. "Yes, you are right on all scores. The author of *No Boundaries* was essentially trying to get people to recognize that the first and most fundamental boundary we establish is that of our skin. What is inside our skin is 'me' and what is outside our skin is 'not me.' Separateness and difference are exactly what makes loving other people so hard. He postulates a sort of 'no-boundary existence' where we recognize that the sameness is far greater than the difference."

Chad was really getting into it. He spit out the words as though he couldn't say them quick enough. "But isn't this similar to what Paul is saying when he uses the analogy of the body of Christ?[10] When the hand hurts, the eye hurts too?"

"Ding ding ding ding, you score again. You still remember that from your church days, huh?" I was impressed.

"Ron, let me get this right. Part of the infection, according to the Christian version, is that we have this boundary-building drive, a desire to judge and to erect artificial and superficial barriers that break down relationships instead of connecting us? Is that a fair assessment?"

"Yes, Chad," I replied. "We tend to think it's OK to give preferential treatment to some and to ignore others. But when Jesus says things like, 'Love your neighbor as yourself,' he doesn't leave much room for distinguishing the lovable from the unlovable."

Heading East

Chad latched on to the idea of infection and boundaries. Frederica Mathewes-Green makes several distinctions that may give us new insights into the human dilemma. She argues that in Western Christianity we've tended to conceive of sin as an *infraction*, while in the Eastern tradition of Christianity sin is an *infection*:

> In the Eastern Orthodox Church, we speak of the impulses that move us toward any kind of sin as "passions." You shouldn't think of this term as related to "passionate." It's more like "passive" (as in "the Passion of Christ"; his passion is what he endured).
>
> These impulses beat us up. They originate as thoughts, sometimes as thoughts that evade full consciousness. The roots are tangled with memories, shame, anger, fear — and the thoughts are also very often inaccurate.
>
> All this mess damages our ability to see the world clearly. We go on misreading situations and other people, and venture further into confusion. The illness compounds itself, to the delight of the Evil One, who nurtures lies and has no compassion on the weak. To him, the weak are breakfast.
>
> Eastern Christianity speaks of this as the darkening of the *nous*, that is, of the perceptive center of a person. (Most English Bibles translate *nous* as *mind*, but that's not quite it;

the *nous* is not the rational intellect but a perceiving faculty. Thoughts and emotions are subsequent reactions to the *nous*'s perceptions.) The damaged *nous* is like a pair of glasses fitted with distorting lenses. It needs healing.

The Greek word represented by this kind of "passion" is *pathos*. It means "suffering." It is because we are helpless in our suffering that Christ came. He took on vulnerable human form and went into the realm of death and defeated the Evil One. Now we are invited to gradually return to health by fully assimilating the truth that sets us free — by assimilating the presence and life of Christ himself. "It is no longer I who live, but Christ who lives in me," St. Paul said. This life fills and changes us like fire fills a piece of coal.

In the Eastern Christian understanding, sins are not "bad deeds" that must be made up in order to satisfy justice. They are instead like bad fruit, which indicates a sickness inside the tree (the analogy Jesus uses in Matthew 7:7–8). Sin is infection, not infraction. And God not only forgives freely but also sent his Son to rescue us when we were helpless.[11]

When sin is viewed as an infraction, as it is in the Western Protestant tradition, we can be led to believe that once the legal transaction for the infraction is taken care of, things are fine. And in a legal setting, where infraction is breaking the law, that is a fine metaphor. But sin is more than a legal issue. This is what we see in the garden when Adam and Eve run and hide from God. They have been infected with a sense of shame, and shame is not dominantly a legal condition but a relational one. Something happened inside themselves, between themselves, and between them and God.

I wonder if this legal/infraction metaphor may be at least partly responsible for the huge letdown many people experience when they begin to follow Christ. The dramatic life change, often promised on the front end, is rarely experienced on the back end.

When we look at the human story after the fall, we see the battle raging between benevolence and selfishness. Selfless, loving, and creative service is hard to come by. These aren't legal issues but relational ones. Many people instantly understand how challenging it is to live in benevolent and creative service to other people. When you talk about an infection of selfishness, they can see it in themselves—just as Chad could—even when they can't see how they have broken a cosmic law for which "the Other" is going to come down hard on them. The idea of us being infected with selfishness and judgmentalism seems a resonant conversation; the idea of us having committed an infraction and angered a holy God does not.

In every manifestation of the infection first experienced by Adam and Eve, we see a shift from selfless to selfish—an intense, often vicious ill will or spite. Read the biblical story carefully, and you'll see case study after case study, example after example, of this intense ill will—the prototype being the story of Cain and Abel in Genesis 4. One can hardly think of a more quintessential story of vicious ill will and violent spite than this sad sequence. The issue at center stage again is *relational*.

This fuller understanding of the creation story and beyond is an essential component of connecting with people on the spiritual conversation level. It helps frame why Jesus came. What if Jesus came because the infection often overwhelms,[12] and he had to provide not only a flesh-and-blood example of what benevolent and creative service and shalom bringing looks like, but also bring a cure or antidote for the infection, so that the "I no longer live, but Christ lives in me" of Galatians 2:20 can be seen. Here again is one of those 1P passages—Jesus, the Son of God, living in a person to such a large degree that Paul can say that he, Paul, doesn't live, but rather it is as if Jesus, the Son of God, is the one living and the one being seen.

Since that day in the checkout lane when my judger gene spoke so loudly I could finally hear it, I can say I haven't been the same. I can't say that I've stopped being a judgmental person, that I don't struggle with it anymore. I *do* try, I *am* more aware, I am *most of the time* alert to that voice when it tries to speak. But I am by no means over my judger infection. My judger gene is what separates me from others; it puts distance between me and other *imago dei* handmade pieces. Judgment rising in me fuels pride and arrogance, which in turn breeds superiority. But here is the good news: I am being cured. I am getting better, and I have taken and continue to take the antibiotic that will ultimately make me well. Jesus lives in me, so ego has no voice.

CHAPTER 7

Fresh Infusion

Rosemary-infused syrup poured over lemon granita is just about the best summer dessert to eat after a great cookout. A large bunch of rosemary is thrown in a hot water/sugar mixture. If you let the rosemary sit, the flavor will slowly but surely permeate the fluid—and you have one delicious dessert item. In an effective infusion, one substance is thoroughly assimilated into another.

We might say that the human flesh God had fashioned from the soil of the earth was infused with his breath, and hence it came to life. When we look at passages such as 1 Corinthians 6:19; Galatians 2:20; and 2 Peter 1:3–4, we see that most of the passages about God dwelling in us are directed at Christ-followers. John 10:34–36, though, and other passages clearly were not addressed to believers but to Jesus' opponents. I wonder if these are New Testament "fresh infusions" to the *imago dei* we see in Genesis 1. It is God's breath/wind/spirit[1] that is hovering over the face of the deep, and it is the breath of God breathed into Adam that imparts *to* him and imprints *in* him the image of God. The obvious and fair conclusion is that everyone on the planet has this original infusion connecting them to God. Every person has the breath/spirit of God in them.[2] When we come to the New Testament, we recognize that the Spirit of God, still viewed as wind/breath/spirit,[3] blows into and around all human beings and has a personal relationship with those who desire it.[4] The Spirit infusing the first creation in Adam is the same Spirit infusing the second, or new, creation.

Can we see this as a fresh infusion to what already exists in every person? Is it possible to see this fresh infusion of Spirit as what reflavors the lives of those who follow Christ?

Jesus provided the perfect functional example and model of how a human can perfectly and fully live out the *imago dei* and lovingly and creatively live out the mission of serving the world. He demonstrated what it means to be a shalom bringer. Jesus came and successfully did what Adam and Eve were originally supposed to do. And he did it all infused with the very same Spirit available to us.

God bestows on humanity the honor of creatively tending, keeping, working, molding, shaping, and naming creation—a God-given charge to be the servant of the world, to be God's representative to and in the creation. Human beings are to represent God to each other and to the rest of creation on God's behalf. This is a remarkable mission that may provide insight into why God created humanity. In lieu of God's erecting a stone statue or wood-hewn pillar representing himself, he chose three-dimensional living, breathing beings who were more than robots executing a computer program but were codesigners in the truest sense of the word. Adam and Eve were to be the image and likeness bearers, showing that they were meant to be benevolent and creative keepers of the world God created. They were to maintain a wholeness in the creation—a shalom, a wellness and completeness that represented the one whose image they bore.

Maintaining wholeness in the world was a mandate given to the human race way back in the garden of Eden. Adam and Eve were given this charge far from the New Testament infusion of the Holy Spirit and power of Jesus. In other words, if you live on the planet, you have been charged with shalom bringing. It is a point of commonality we all share. I wonder if the breath of God, clearly the Spirit of God, breathed into Adam and Eve, and this imparting to them of the *imago dei* isn't simply the raw material, so to speak, that is augmented, added to, and updated by the same Holy Spirit talked about in the New Testament.

The breath of God we receive in our first breath out of the womb is never fully satisfying until the operating system gets the system upgrade from the same Spirit. The John 3 Nicodemus story may be the best illustration of these elements coming together. When we receive the Holy Spirit — when we are born again and undergo the paradigm shift that Nicodemus experienced — aren't we re-receiving, or receiving more, or entering into a new relationship, or getting an operating system update? These are all just metaphors, but there seems to be a connection between *imago dei* and the reception of the Spirit in the New Testament. When we get our spiritual upgrade, we are being reacquainted with how we were originally created and taken even further in our journey. When we follow Jesus to the acceptance of our mission to be servants of others and the created world, we are updating in a flesh-and-blood example what we were supposed to be doing from the very beginning by living as *imago dei*.

From Conquest to Conversation

In theological discussions, we often talk about creation/new creation parallels. Aren't these new and old connections something we should reflect on more if we want to be effective in this area of spiritual conversations? The original breath of God given to all people is rebreathed or reinfused in Jesus. Our interior architecture is designed to need this reinfusion. Spiritual conversations are supposed to point in the direction of where the reinfusion can be found.

Isn't this infusion the very thing predicted by the prophet Joel as he quotes the Lord: "I will pour out my Spirit on *all* people" (Joel 2:28, italics added)? Isn't this another new breath of God on all humanity? The use of Joel 2 in Peter's message in Acts 2 strengthens this metaphor tie-in. The accompanying "sound like the blowing of a violent wind" can hardly be coincidental (Acts 2:2.) The Spirit of God and the interplay of the metaphor of wind and breath seem to tie the first (old) and second (new) creations together.

Just as rosemary changes the flavor of the sugar syrup it is infusing, our story will change when it is laid inside the larger, grander, more compelling and completing story of God. Exploration of this sort is now bringing us to the very reason Jesus comes on the scene.

A fuller understanding of the story will change the conversation with those interested in starting the journey. As we've seen, when we start the story with the fall narrative, omitting the background of *imago dei*, we have a relatively propositional, transactional, and infraction-oriented conversation. We have to consider this as we figure out how to tell a more complete story. When we invite people to come to Jesus through a transaction of buying into certain propositions and reciting a prayer, the mechanical feel of such an exchange makes it hard to feel as though we are entering into a relationship. And yet within the Christian church we continue to affirm that it's all about relationships, not rules. But is it really? Are our metaphors and approaches relational, or more about winning someone over and keeping rules and boundaries?

The metaphors of conquest, winning, crusade (as in "evangelistic crusade"), battle — and pet phrases such as "the lost," "get them to surrender," and a host of others — instantly draw lines of who is in and who is out, friends and foes, enemies and family. These aren't graphic overstatements unfairly depicting conservative Christianity; these are the words and phrases we use to represent our construct of what we think Jesus wants us to do.

We feel totally justified in our use of this narrow militant imagery. Why? Because we are certain we have the one, complete, totally accurate picture. Ironically, we get very concerned when Islamic fundamentalists use the same imagery. We question its propriety, express our concern, and become outraged. The obvious arrogance we exhibit before the rest of the world with our smug certainty is one of the reasons we struggle to engage in credible spiritual conversations.

These sorts of metaphors not only make spiritual conversations hard; they lead to a point-of-sale understanding of conversion and a certain type of evangelistic training equipped only for that type of transactional conversion. We have a domino effect to deal with here. A fall-redemption theological starting point — a primarily infraction and propositional understanding of sin and Jesus' reason for coming — will lead us to certain types of metaphors and understandings of conversion. With this type of understanding of conversion, it is obvious that it will drive the method of evangelism and the way we train people to do it.

That Was Relational, not Rational

Apologetics is one further ripple in the pond we must consider. For the last several decades of the twentieth century, apologetics was an enterprise largely built around the scientific model of garnering evidence for the purpose of persuasion. We should affirm a role for persuasion as a way to point people to an understanding of God and who Jesus is,[5] but when we look at the dominant emphasis in evangelical circles for those decades, we find a model that plays by the rules of a modernist, scientific worldview. She with the biggest pile of evidence wins. Those decades show a church co-opted by the spirit of the age and the building of a system bound to pass as the cultural shifts from modernism to postmodernism take root.

Even the evidentialists who were using evidence to persuade were quick to add, "You can never prove beyond a shadow of a doubt that there is a God, or who Jesus is, because that would take all the faith out of it." In essence, they concluded, we are dealing in probabilities.

Here is the problem though: faith doesn't broker in the realm of probabilities or possibilities. Faith is relational; evidence is propositional. Faith can hold paradox; evidence is clear. One more time we find ourselves in the arena of propositions, proofs, and mounds of evidence—hardly the thing you would find compelling about entering a relationship with anyone, let alone God. Relationship has mysterious dimensions, uncertain starting points, fluid categories. When I recently asked a guy when his relationship with his wife started, he was stopped dead in his tracks. When asked if he knew if he was in fact in relationship with her, he was absolutely certain. When I further queried if he had any proof of the existence of the relationship, he admitted that it was all about a shared commitment to love. He was most intrigued, though, by the "when" question: When did your relationship start? When you first laid eyes on her? First date? First kiss? When?

While entering a relationship with God via propositional buy-in doesn't sound too enticing, the dilemma is even acuter these days. In our postmodern world, evidence and persuasion of the modern world type are rather suspect. They are perceived as power plays and tactical artifacts of a yesteryear world. I'm not sure what your experience is, but the kinds of questions spiritual questioners were asking me fifteen years ago are far different from the questions I'm asked today. Two decades ago, spouting the number of biblical scrolls in existence and their approximate dates might have been greeted with oohs and aahs—but not anymore.

Postmodern pluralism has caused the questions to shift to an entirely different arena, and the conversation to change. The existence of God doesn't seem to be nearly as mainstream a question as it used to be; it is, for the most part, assumed (I recognize, however, that there has been a spate of recent books about God from atheistic and agnostic positions). The Bible as a sacred document isn't up for debate; many people outside of Christianity are OK with that premise (as many Christians can value other sacred texts). That Jesus is in some way a "pretty unique" figure (I know it's oxymoronic, but it's definitely where our culture sits) is hardly questioned. No longer is the question, "*Does* God exist? but "*Which* god do I believe in?" No longer is the question, "How can I know that the Bible is reliable?" but "Is the Bible any more sacred than the Upanishads or the Qur'an?" And many people are able to say, "I'm all in on the historical Jesus, but I find Gandhi helpful, as well as the Sufi mystic Tukaram."

Many of these questions have shifted because we now personally know Buddhists, Hindus, and Muslims. Our kids play Xbox after school with kids who are from Malaysia, Korea, India, and China. The general population's education, or at least awareness, about these other world religions makes the issues far more complex and requires something far more winsome than evidence.

On Dialogue and Conversation

So what practical adjustments should we consider if we are to engage in true dialogue? Possibly the biggest practical difference between the old evangelism model and the spiritual conversation model is the movement from *telling and selling and a moment in time* to *questioning and conversing and a process through time*. The old evangelism model assumes that we have all the right answers, and we're trying to sell these answers. Unfortunately, in this case we listen to the other person in order to carry out a better sales presentation, and at times we can come off as condescending. This evaluation sounds crass and a bit harsh, but it is a reasonably fair representation of what happens. From diagrams on napkins to tract booklets and the four spiritual laws (all extracted from the context in which they were originally housed), the evangelism model of old is point of sale, and the goal is to close it as quickly as possible, because "today is the day of salvation."

Another significant difference—one that will become a major focus of the next section—is the shift from evidence and argument as a way to persuade, toward conversations around the issue of our transformational architecture. I'd like to see us begin spiritual conversations with attention to universal spiritual DNA components, not the use of evidence that is susceptible to being overturned (by means of new evidence yet to be discovered), unavailable (to a tribe in India, let's say), and in most cases only usable in literate cultures.

When we start with our deepest passions rooted in *imago dei*, we are at a place universal in availability and incontrovertible with evidence—because *imago dei* is in every human heart and is postliterate (not requiring any education, library, or special knowledge to engage), cross-cultural (all locations), and trans-temporal (all time periods of history). The tribal man in the region of Assam in India has no books or evidence at his disposal for evaluation, but he does have the deepest passions in the core of his being. A high school dropout single mom in a New York ghetto may not be able to navigate complex arguments about evidence for the existence of God, but she does have the promptings of *imago dei*. No matter who or where you are, everyone has the same yearnings designed at their core. This is as true for a remote tribeswoman in Kenya as a business executive in Brussels, a poor mother in a barrio in Brazil, or a gang member in downtown Bangkok. Targeting a message and model that can engage all of these situations seems to be an issue we should learn more about.

The Common Grill Conversations

Chad and I had missed a couple of our twilight outings, and this particular week it was raining, so when I got a phone call from him, I wasn't surprised.

"Hey, Ron, how 'bout we meet in Chelsea at The Common Grill and have some seafood and a little dialogue. Sound good?"

An hour and a half later, he and I were sitting in one of the great restaurants in this part of central Michigan. Today was my turn to set the agenda, and I wanted to learn from Chad. My business card may read "consultant," but more often than not I'm a consultee. I don't have all the answers, and when I readily acknowledge that I have a lot to learn from guys like Chad, our interchanges become tremendous growth catalysts for me.

"Here's what I have been wondering about," I said. "What is your spiritual journey like? Does *spiritual journey* even have any resonance with you, any point of reference? I know you don't consider yourself a Christian, and my question isn't about that. But how would you characterize whatever this spiritual interest you're expressing is all about? Where does it come from? What drives it? What happens inside of you as you are exploring? Can you give me any insight on any of that?"

The waitress dropped off the basket containing the best bread imaginable. Plenty of butter and a couple baskets of this bread, and I can say, "Check, please."

"That's a great question," Chad said. 'I told you I grew up in the church, left it all in college, and have never felt even one compelling reason to return. But as I also said, I do find the life of Jesus compelling. I find the life of Gandhi compelling. I just don't find the institutions compelling. But I think I'm able to say it's deeper than that."

Chad seemed open to exploring this, so I took another step down the road. "OK, good. That is what I wanted to get at. Let's leave the institution aside for a minute. Let me hear your take on what you find so compelling about Jesus or Gandhi and—" I didn't get to finish. The waitress came over and wanted to tell us the menu specials. I'm not sure what they all were, but the one that echoed in my ears was shredded lobster claw tossed with fettuccine and red bell pepper cream and fresh rosemary. At that stage, anything else she said was superfluous; I knew what I was having.

After she took our order, Chad began to explore my question. "From the perspective of one who has been on the inside and outside, it seems to me that the church has no room for process, no room for exploration—for a pace that allows you to really explore. And maybe that shouldn't happen in the church, but it should be able to happen with church people!" We both grabbed another piece of bread, emptying the basket—except for the black poppy seeds in the bottom. Chad looked at me and made a motion with his head that signaled the need for more bread. "I guess if I had to characterize my journey, and I don't know if this will answer your question, it really is a slow process. I feel faith growing in me, or it's regrowing, or I'm getting reacquainted with it—but I would say it isn't enhanced by nailing down all sorts of doctrinal specifics. Does that make sense?"

I was nodding my head and just trying to be fully present and track with his concerns. I had never emerged from our time together being disappointed for having paid close attention. "And by 'explore' you mean—?" I asked.

"Well, I guess I mean that I have all sorts of questions about the current 'brand' of Christianity that is out there. Does it really reflect the Jesus I learned about in the Gospels as I grew up and whom I've come to read more about as an adult? I've tried asking this question in a couple of churches I visited right out of college, but there was no tolerance for that. And in some ways I understand the threat that poses. The thing is, I'm really not trying to beat up on the church per se, or on any particular Christian group."

"Sure," I said as I sucked on my straw and heard the gurgle at the bottom of the glass as it drained. "You mentioned doctrinal specifics and faith. Elaborate. How are you saying those do or do not fit together?" I flagged our waitress as she whisked by, and I whispered, "Another coke with Rose's lime juice, please."

Chad continued. "I look at what the disciples had to believe as they followed Jesus, and it couldn't have been much. Most of the dogma the church has pushed at people is stuff developed well past the time Jesus walked on this earth." As Chad kept talking, I kept nodding my head. "The church seems to have more concern about people having the right doctrinal starting point than Jesus did. Jesus seems relational in his starting point, not rational."

"Chad, that's a gem of a line. How did you say it? Jesus is more interested in the relational than the rational, or he has a relational starting point, not a rational one?"

"Close enough," Chad said. "That's the gist of it." Salads arrived, along with another basket of bread—and was it ever hot and fresh! Chad smiled at the waitress and thanked her. He went on. "I recognize I'm somewhat anti-institutional. But I don't know any of my friends and colleagues who aren't. And it's not just church; it's a lot of institutions. Our parents dragged us to church most Sundays when we were growing up, but none of us give a flip about any of it today. And none of us want our kids subjected to the narrow, bigoted, and arrogant party line you have to parrot to attend most churches. And yet I'll say it again, most of us are in relationships with other people or groups of people where spiritual conversations like the ones you and I have are going on."

He paused long enough to find the pepper hidden behind the wine list. I asked, "What do you think people are looking for or are interested in that makes them willing to take time out of their busy lives to pursue this sort of thing—to have these spiritual conversations with those you're hanging out with?"

"That's easy for me. I won't speak for others, but I imagine they feel somewhat similar. We want to find direction for this sense of connection to something larger than ourselves, and we want camaraderie as we do it. We want to help the world, and we're convinced that spirituality is part of the solution."

"I can buy that," I said. "I hear that often."

"And you know, Ron," Chad said, "the people I know are *so* open. They are well-read and intelligent, and yet they're turned off by the in/out, black/white of most churches. That's what it's like with that old 'world evangelism' thing. It is black and white, either/or, right or wrong—and if you don't follow the prescription down to a tee, you are just out of luck. And I have to say that whole approach is very infantile and close-minded, and frankly in any other area of life it would be considered uncharitable and bigoted. But in the church it seems to be a glaring blind spot. But I have to be careful, because I recognize that I don't know a ton of churches. I realize that this is *my* experience and may not be a very good representative sample. It's what I happen to see from my seat, however."

"Help me get at what you see as the alternative to this blind spot," I said.

The waitstaff helper who was clearing tables came by and removed our salad plates to make way for the arrival of our main course.

"Well, for me it is at the very least a recognition that everybody really is in a process of discovery. I have gone back and read the Gospels at length since leaving the church in college, and it seems that the disciples were quite dense, in a constant process of discovery, often confused and uncertain, and always asking inane and at times downright—at least what appears to me to be—stupid questions. The disciples never seem to be given an ultimatum by Jesus, such as, 'Here are the beliefs you have to buy, and if you can just sign on the dotted line, I would love to have you follow me.'"

I just nodded my approval and said, "Fair enough."

"So much of what the church pushes on people is material, doctrine, dogma—developed much later than the New Testament, and yet if you listen to pastors and church people talk, they make it sound like all that stuff comes right from the mouth of Jesus. I've often thought it would be really interesting to have a conversation about whether or not Jesus would believe some of the things churches believe or make you believe to become a member."

Chad paused long enough to take a last bite of bread and then continued. "This is one of the reasons I find the ideas of people like Karen Armstrong so attractive. She really believes that Christianity and other world religions have added into the mix certain things that their founders wouldn't identify, and that therefore these religions face the threat of being made irrelevant by the very organism that is to be their mouthpiece."

Chad reached for his glass to take a sip of Coke and pick up his napkin that had fallen on the floor.

"I totally hear what you're saying," I said. "In the church we haven't been good at acknowledging process; it is one of those all-or-nothing propositions. I have to apologize to you because one of the things I'm seeing in my own life is that after nearly thirty years of being a Christian, I am on far more of a journey of discovery today than I realized even ten years ago. Maybe what I'm saying is that I hope I am less arrogant now. I don't know how much of this is a function of age and maturity, but I think this observation in my own life is not something I would have made when I was twenty-five or thirty." I cringed at the memories of some of my less-than-gracious acts. "A number of times recently I have apologized from the pulpit to first-time visitors who hadn't set foot in a church in years because they had been so turned off by people like me and the people I was trying to encourage."

Just then two plates of steaming food were delivered. What an aroma—rosemary and steamy red bell pepper cream! After the food had been placed in front of us, Chad waited for me to finish the thought.

"What I was just about to say was, I hope age is deflating arrogance and unjustified certainty. I honestly think that is growth for me."

Chad picked up on that statement. "That may be true, but I think it can go both ways. I know guys who get more entrenched, certain, and condescending the older they get. So I'm not sure it's a function of age. I do think a lot of it has to do with the value we place on certainty. I know as I went through high school and college and even in my job, everything seemed to be about being sure, being certain, knowing beyond the shadow of a doubt. Can you honestly take that tack heading into a spiritual journey and still really be honest when things aren't clear and certain? Come on, we're dealing with God here and with people's understandings and experiences with God. There's so much that is a mystery."

"That's a great point," I said. "It's hard to be honest about misgivings and doubts when the default commitment is certainty, an 'I have it all together' aura. It's so helpful in my personal journey in our learning community that we can really express where we sit, questions and all. Chad, this is really great stuff for me to learn from you. Your observations about certainty are worth thinking about some more. I realize that this attitude of certainty propped up a whole lot of my speaking and teaching ministry. The crazy part of that is how for me certainty was quietly but definitely linked to control. If I could be certain, then I could legitimately draw lines of who is in and who is out. And certainty leading to control results in everybody who is as certain as I am about what I deem to be important being "in." I have had to recognize that I was caught in a vicious circle. And yet I haven't had to become an agnostic. I simply have a chastened—and I think more realistic—view of my rationality. When that view is present, I think humility grows."

Chad was nodding his head as he swallowed a mouthful of food. "That's the point right there, Ron. If we could just carry on conversations about the journey each of us is on, with the effort to learn from each other but not try to convert each other, I'm guessing there would be a lot of progress toward people beginning to experience deep personal change."

Vocabulary

Our discussion on the shift in story and starting point has been a necessary prerequisite work for coming to grips with just how different the "methodology of evangelism" must be as well. I use quotation marks because a method of evangelism does nothing but betray just how much a product of the modern world our whole approach has been. In some ways, all methods are born of the era in which they find themselves. The problem, of course, is canonizing a particular method as if it could be useful for all time. Having laid the initial groundwork for a shift in the story and starting point, we can now reflect on how these shifts create a different type of spiritual interchange.

Let's further explore the subtle but important shift that takes place when we move from evangelism to spiritual conversation. To move toward a "process and discovery" view of things instead of the old modern point-of-sale model is a decided shift. I am afraid that with the baggage the words *evangelist* and *evangelism* bring, coupled with the fact that companies such as Nike often use the word *evangelist* to describe a product salesperson, the word has lost its usefulness, at least in the short term.[6]

Every time I have used the word *evangelist* or *evangelism* in the presence of a church outsider, the cringe factor was immense. The freight they have associated with the word is enough to convince me to strike the word from my everyday vocabulary. The goal isn't to simply add new words that reflect the same old definitions we've always had. If we were to do that, we would be treading far too close to bait-and-switch territory in my opinion.

My hope in altering vocabulary is to allow us to redefine, more fully define, and in some cases more accurately define the terms of the conversation. When new and unfamiliar words are used, we are given the opportunity to invest these terms with the meanings we want to become a part of the conversation. When I use a volatile word in a church circle—with churched people—they assume they know what I'm referring to, and so a redefinition is tough to pull off. In other words, I can try to redefine evangelism to a group of church people all I want, but I have news for you: that word is so defined and freighted it doesn't matter what I say; the current definitional baggage is going to win the day—which is why I vote for using another phrase.

Finally Getting Somewhere

When we begin to make these adjustments in our understandings and in how we carry on conversations, all sorts of cool things start to happen. Here is an excerpt from an email I received from a woman who attended a conference I presented in Arizona:

Dear Ron,

I don't know if you'll remember me, but I was at the conference you did here in Scottsdale. I am a short Hispanic woman named Tula you met out in the lobby. I just had to tell you what has happened. You are not going to believe it! I grew up in a conservative Baptist church. All I have known is the traditional "present the gospel and give an altar call" message. I admit that when I heard you, I was a bit skeptical but realized that what you had said at the beginning of the day was true for me. I have ideas that are very set in stone and won't change anytime soon unless I am willing to examine whether the ideas I have are really serving me well or need to be revised. Well, I will get to the main point I want to share because I *have* changed — and that change in me has already brought about fruit.

My sister and her husband are now on the journey to follow Jesus! I had talked to them before. But they had been turned off by going to church with me and by the way I have approached them. I actually went home and asked them to forgive me and told them I too was on a journey and had learned some new things that were changing the way I thought about how we come to follow Jesus. (Ron, I came to Christ through my old Catholic grandmother praying for me and trying to get me to go to Mass. It was never a big "point-of-sale thing," to use your words. Why I would force that on my sister and brother-in-law shows how blind I was to my own way of doing things.) My sharing with them my new understandings and asking them to forgive my arrogance were the things that put them in the position to say they want to explore this. You can't know how happy I am for my family and for the others I hope to share this with in the future. I just had to let you know.

In Christ,
Tula

CHAPTER 8

Our Lost Story Chapters

I was at a church a while ago to lead a theology class for the entire church. We were discussing how to reevaluate our personal story in light of God's story and to let the "God version" begin to have a little louder volume. I had a deluge of comments when we were done, but one in particular stood out.

Chris came up, with tears streaming down her face. "I have been sober now for twenty-one years, but I have never gotten past my alcoholic days as the primary definer of who I am," she said. "Tonight something snapped inside of me. What I realize is that I can choose what story to tell, and if I continue to tell the incomplete story of my brokenness instead of the *imago dei* piece of God's story, then I'm simply highlighting the wrong thing as the primary part of my story. I have been using a sad chapter in my story and telling it to myself as if it is the outcome and whole of the story."

She began to give me some background on how she had arrived at this place in her journey: "Ron, I didn't grow up in the church. I got involved in alcohol and drugs in college, and before I knew it, I was married and had two kids. The real awakening came when I woke up one Wednesday morning so hungover I could hardly move. The sad thing was, I was sick as a dog not because of some party the night before but because my daily drinking was such a huge problem. I realized right then that I was in deep trouble."

"So what did you do?"

"I had some well-meaning friends invite me to their church. They assured me that a lot of this was simply 'sin stuff' in my life and if I 'got saved' " — she made quote marks with her hands — "everything would start to get on track. But you know what? It wasn't true! All I ended up with was a much greater sense of guilt. Getting saved didn't alleviate any guilt I felt for my problem, and if anything, it made me feel like more of a failure."

"Chris, I'm sorry. We often do things in the church we think will help, but we don't always do a great job."

She looked at me. "Ron, all those people had good hearts. And I hate to say it this way, but I needed more than simply getting saved; I needed a new story. I couldn't even find that through AA. I have been sober for twenty-one years — but broken all the same. Nothing has actually changed what I'm feeling deep down inside."

Chris had stopped sobbing as she began to tell her story to me, but right at this point she obviously felt touched again because her tears started to freely flow again. "This is my night of real healing. Realizing that I have been telling myself the wrong story, that I have been emphasizing Genesis 3, not Genesis 1. I have an iPod in my head playing the wrong story. I'm sorry, but this is just overwhelming to me. What a night, what a night!"

We had a rich exchange as she realized how powerful it is in our journey to make sure we are selecting ways of fitting together all of the pieces of our story. Her conversion and reorientation continued that night.

Accidental or Intentional Deletions?

The idea of spiritual conversations reveals the process and discovery of what coming to follow Jesus is all about. When we look at what happened with the disciples and when we examine our own lives, the *process* and *journey* dimensions seem far more appropriate to the idea of spiritual conversations than the word *evangelism*, which is laden with negatives. But there may be something far more important, something that has to do with the whole point and purpose of spiritual conversations/evangelism in the first place.

The late Australian social worker Michael White and his colleague David Epston help us come to grips with what Chris was describing. We choose the stories that define ourselves. Their book, *Narrative Means to Therapeutic Ends*, is fascinating and contains important insights into the whole idea of conversation. The starting point is in the conversations we have with ourselves. Narrative therapy is built on the premise that how we define ourselves emerges from the stories we select out of our experience to reiterate to ourselves and then to others. In other words, our understanding of ourselves is highly selective, and of course it can't be otherwise. For a whole host of reasons, we select—which means we also deselect—stories that we tell ourselves about ourselves, and we live out of the framework of that story.[1]

Narrative therapists try to help people recognize that they can undergo dramatic change by telling other stories within their experience or by balancing the stories they tell themselves with alternative interpretations of these stories. If you've felt abandoned your whole life due to one painful incident that has loomed larger than life in your own self-definition, what could happen as the one story is told from a different vantage point or is muted and balanced by a whole host of untold or "unstoried" stories in your experience? Is it possible that after hearing more stories or differing interpretations of the ones you tell, maybe you weren't abandoned at all? Powerful, huh?

Reshaping

What is the point of all of this when it comes to spiritual conversations? Part of what we are trying to do in these conversations is draw out a person's journey—his or her spiritual path to date, the mile markers along the way. But when we invite people to be disciples of Jesus, we're ultimately encouraging them to let their personal story be reshaped by God's story. Chris was deeply moved because even though she was part of the family of Christ, she was stuck telling herself an incomplete story. That night, Chris was invited to let the full biblical story become the defining story of her life, and as a result she received permission to give up other stories that had shaped her life in false or distorting ways. In chapter 3 I identified one shaping story we've all been influenced by, namely, the American Dream story. Add into the drive and tension of that plot all the personal dynamics of upbringing and family life, and you are bound to find some brokenness and distortion.

In spiritual conversations we want to help people see how an alternative story, the biblical story, can reshape and remold life in a way that returns to the wholeness of the garden of Eden. For only in the garden can our deepest yearnings can be satisfied. Only in the garden can our lives be reshaped by the narrative God has designed us to live from the very beginning. Inherent in all of this is the idea of *conversion*.

Some people will balk because this doesn't seem centered on Jesus enough. It is unfortunate they see it this way because Jesus *is* at the center of the story, but he, in fact, isn't the whole story. If you need something that has Jesus more at the center, let me give you the definition of my mentor Scot McKnight: "Conversion is the process of identity formation in which the person comes to see himself or herself in accordance with the gospel of Jesus Christ."[2] I might even expand on Scot's definition to say, "Conversion is the process of reorienting and reshaping your life around God's story and the lordship of Jesus." Reorientation here points to a redirectioning; reshaping points to the indelible marking of a life once the direction has changed.

I can't overstate how important these definitions are. Both address the key issue of a redefining of our lives and a shift in the source of that definition. When our identity shifts from being defined by all sorts of self-interest, achievement, income, titles, family — and a host of other things — to who we were made to be in the garden of Eden, brought alive and energized fully by the life, death, and resurrection of Jesus, we are undergoing conversion.

Both *reorienting* and *reshaping* have inherent in them a sense of process, a sense of shift, a sense of journey. The idea of conversion, while certainly commencing at a point in time, is something that is ongoing throughout a lifetime. Scot McKnight again: "The latent emphasis on a one-time decision settling for all time the issues is also worthy of criticism.... Jesus gives absolutely no attention to 'the big decision' or to a single-event conversion. Instead he continues to call the same group of followers to renew their commitment to following him in love, service, and obedience."[3]

Reconnecting Our Missing Chapters

To continue with the insights of narrative therapy in understanding others' personal spiritual journeys, our task is to hear the stories they select to tell themselves and thereby give shape to their self-understanding. We can give no judgment about the validity or veracity of these stories, only that they are primary elements in constructing a person's self-understanding. And we can introduce them to a larger, more encompassing, more elegant story—and invite them to see themselves in that story.

When people have selected stories from their experience that constantly illustrate (to themselves) that they aren't valued, have little to contribute, and have little chance of ever amounting to much, they develop a deeply entrenched story line. In the fall-redemption model of storying the Christian message, we would affirm their basic story and let them know that they *are* indeed deeply defective—people we call "sinners."

Unfortunately, often before we get to the "good news"—in Jesus all of this can be healed—we have shut down the conversation. It's easy to see why. We started with bad news. When we start the conversation with an individual's own self-understanding, we have a far better chance of helping him or her see how God's story can reshape and remold their personal story.

If we start the conversation in creation and not fall, that's the kind of conversation that results. When we talk about how they have been made in the image of God and are actually designed and built with deep yearnings that when fulfilled are deeply satisfying, we not only provide a different starting point for the typical evangelistic conversation; we provide the setting for a result that is dramatically different from most people's self-talk. And if we can help people move from telling themselves limiting and broken stories about who they are, we are moving them precisely in the direction of reorientation.

I hope you can hear what's going on here. I am not suggesting that people do not have the ability to identify strengths and weaknesses and see their wrongdoings and shortcomings. What is clear, though, is that issues of worth, value, and self-understanding can be molded by stories we select and then give far too much airplay to in our heads. When these dysfunctional, self-defining stories are deselected from the playlist, and in their place God's bigger story is inserted, we begin to see the possibility for dramatic healing and change.

God's Big Fat Story

God's story is the overarching and true story about our lives and about the history, trajectory, and goal of his creation. When we do not let his story define, shape, and mold our secondary stories or subplots, then we are living in distorted, murky, and incomplete narratives. God's narrative has the power to reconstruct our lives. God's story has in it the necessary elements for me to slowly but surely learn to see myself as God sees me.

We need to embrace God's overarching story — a story that didn't start with Jesus or with the events of the New Testament. The Old Testament story isn't simply a dry, dusty, dispensable warm-up band for the main concert. It is part of the plot and story line necessary to understand God's original intention in creation and his reason for creating humanity in the first place. Jesus' role in the whole plan is to invite us to be a part of his grand restoration project.

Without knowing God's original intent in the creation program, we would have no way to know what Jesus came to restore. Restoration implies a return *to* something. It isn't coincidental that Revelation 21 looks, smells, and feels an awful lot like Genesis 1 and 2. And just for the record, the picture of the new garden in Revelation 21 isn't *up there* somewhere or *out there* somewhere — it is brought *here* to the earth. Should we be surprised? The direction of the Incarnation is the same as that of the prayer taught by the Incarnate One: downward! "Your kingdom come, your will be done, on earth as it is in heaven."

Concerning the overarching narrative of *both* Testaments, as I've taken the risk to be more honest with myself I've had to conclude that the message isn't what I thought it was for the first twelve to fifteen years of my ministry. I thought the message was fundamentally about getting to heaven—the place we go when we die. But the narrative, read as a whole, seems to be much more about what it means to live in and experience the shalom of God. Life is about experiencing that shalom, brokering it to others, and helping them recognize how their personal narratives are re-formed and reshaped when inserted into the story line of God. That story started with the creation of Adam and Eve and their placement in the garden. The goal of life is to help the cosmos in all of its dimensions be restored to that original creation intention.

Moving to the Inside

Like many nondenominational churches in the 1990s, the church I served told a fall-redemption version of the Christian story. Evangelism was simply about getting current attendees to invite people to the big Sunday event so that the weekend speaker could get people to give their hearts to Jesus. "Invest and Invite!" we would say: *Invest* in some relationships so you could finally *invite* them to church. We pastors, we told them, will take it from there.

This attractional and magnetic model of doing church may be largely responsible for the Barna statistic I cited in chapter 1: "the typical churched believer will die without ever leading one person to become a follower of Jesus." Plenty of people will have invited someone to a weekend church service, but this isn't quite the same.

Our typical altar call wasn't particularly unusual for a church that had drunk deeply at the well of seeker-type paradigms. We didn't have anyone actually come forward to an altar, but we did invite people to raise hands or to seek out someone on the stage or an usher to confirm their decision that day to "follow Christ as their personal Lord and Savior."

Through a series of circumstances we came face-to-face with the reality that a vast majority of people do not come to follow Jesus at a point in time they can mark. Not only did they not experience Jesus in some sort of Pauline blinding light, Damascus road experience; most people didn't even know when they became followers. Our research and informal polling of hundreds of people indicate that most people do not have a determinative date or crisis moment — "here and now is when I decided to follow."

For some people, this is a load of guilt off their shoulders; for others, this statement is tantamount to heresy. In some circles I've been in, if you don't have a date written down in the flyleaf of your Bible, you may not actually be "saved." We had both types on our church staff. Several staff members who were from a Lutheran background were comfortable with the idea of salvation as a process — a written date in the flyleaf of their Bible was nowhere to be found. Some who were raised as Baptists weren't sure which campfire meeting or altar call response represented the moment they "got saved" — in the end, they had to admit that, even given a strong point-of-sale theology, they had come to follow Christ as a process — one they were still in.

The Process

In John 16, Jesus assures us that the Holy Spirit is at work in the heart of every person who doesn't yet know God. Our experience of coming to be "saved" involves a number—sometimes a large number—of interior promptings that slowly prepares, woos, and draws us into relationship with Jesus. These interior promptings are sometimes in the form of quiet impressions or self-conversations in which probing questions are raised, and other times are decisive events and challenges that lead to turning points. These inflection points are small steps on the pathway of redirectioning their lives—step-by-step reorientations, often with little fanfare, that are nonetheless decisive in the long run. As part of the pool of experience, they are responsible for drawing a person into relationship with Jesus. This process is underground and quiet, happening in the interior architecture of the heart.

■

When I ran into Chris the following month, she was stoked. This time there were no tears—only words bubbling from her mouth about something she just had to share with me.

"You're not going to believe what I did with what I learned last month. I took the ideas of *imago dei* and telling yourself the right story and introduced them to my AA group."

I looked at her with wide eyes. "And how did that go over?"

"You're not going to believe this. Six people want to get together every week after our meeting to talk about the stories we tell ourselves and what God's story would suggest. I just can't believe it. I would have never in a million years felt comfortable doing this, but I am so excited. I have people asking me to engage with them in a spiritual journey and conversation. Who would have ever guessed it?"

CHAPTER 9

New Vantage Points

Terry asked if I would have lunch with a couple from his church who were bent on leading the charge for an ecology ministry at his church. He wanted to know my thoughts about ecology as ministry because he was quite sure it wasn't in the Bible. But the big kicker for him was, "I just don't have any idea if they're even Christians."

As we sat down to lunch at Red Robin, Terry introduced me to Paul and Sandy. Yep, pretty much what you would expect of a couple wanting to do ecology ministry, down to the Birkenstocks and huge, pocketed cargo shorts both were wearing. They were in their late fifties, hippies from the word go (their words, I might add). They had tan lines from lots of sun time and obviously were hiker/camper types.

"So, tell me about yourselves. What is the Paul and Sandy story?"

"Well, Ron," Paul started the conversation, "thanks for having lunch with us. Terry tells us you get this ecology thing and thought we could be helped by your insights."

"Paul, you're going to be disappointed because I don't have any insights about the earth and going green. But I *do* help churches set up ministries inside and outside the four walls of the church."

"Perfect. That is exactly what we told Terry we want to do." Sandy pulled out a stack of brochures that I was convinced would be promoting some sort of organization they were involved in but instead contained various outreach ministry listings from Terry's church. Sandy plopped down the brochures and said, "We're hoping that the next time these are printed, there will be a listing about projects to help us clean up and be more sensitive to the earth." As she talked, she looked at Terry, shot him a smile, and then turned her eyes to me.

"You asked about our story. We aren't religious at all, but we are really spiritual. And we are totally cool with Jesus and all, but we aren't totally sold on the church thing yet. I told Paul I didn't think we could just sit around and try to really 'get it' unless we were willing to get involved at some level. So I was the one who said, 'Let's do something in the area of our passion.' We've helped restore the mud turtle habitat over the border in Mexico. We teach bird-watching classes and classes on how to create bird sanctuary spaces. We've helped people begin to be involved in recycling. And we're really interested in water reclamation and hydrology. Ron, we experience God in creation. We haven't yet experienced him in church this same way, but we're willing to help the church if it is willing to let us serve in the areas we're excited about."

Paul continued. "We would love to hear your suggestions. We're not saying we are attending this church to create a platform for ourselves. We already have several of those. That isn't our point. But we would like to get into relationships with people where we can help them on the ecology front and they can maybe help us on the spiritual front. That's what we think real community is about."

As you can imagine, it was a fascinating lunch. Paul and Sandy were incredible people. They had traveled the world and been involved in projects I had never even heard of or could have dreamed up. The ensuing conversation with Terry was really good too. He realized that Paul and Sandy totally get the 3P conversation and that this is just a different vantage point from which he can start the journey conversation. God and Spirit for them are experienced in creation. Failing to build on that already present connection with God or writing it off as New Age or pagan would be to miss one of the ways God shows himself to people.

1P, 2P, 3P

I have already had conversations with Chad, Paul, Sandy, and Terry about 1P, 2P, and 3P understandings of God, distinctions that are helpful in clarifying why certain ideas about God seem easy to talk about and others are off-limits. A quick review: A first person (1P) understanding is God is within me. A second person (2P) understanding is God is out there as "Other" to be related to as a person. And a third person (3P) understanding is God as inhabiting creation — the third person "it" idea. This 1P, 2P, 3P idea isn't just about understandings of God, though. There are three kinds of knowledge, each of which correspond to the 1P, 2P, and 3P distinctions.

1P: When I talk about knowledge of myself, my internal thought world, my feelings, introspection, what happens inside me when I pray, the self-conversations I carry on with myself — all of this is first person knowledge. It is knowledge about *me, my, mine* — all of which are first person pronouns. Seems easy enough, right? The interesting thing is the fact that you are an expert on 1P knowledge, but only *your* 1P knowledge. While you and I can have similar internal experiences, only you know yours and only I know mine. No one can talk you out of 1P knowledge. What happens inside your interior world can't be argued with by someone else — to you it is as real as it gets. I suspect you can quickly see why this first person knowledge is so important to apologetics. Your experience of God is an experience in the 1P arena. We don't have to have proof of it, evidence for it, or tools for assessing its presence.

2P: When I notice "another" (you), and you enter my awareness and I start talk to you, I ask things such as, "How do I know what you mean when you use that phrase or word?" I am identifying a second kind of knowledge (2P). I ask, "Am I extracting from your words what you mean to communicate?" When I ask these questions, I have to draw on a totally different kind of knowledge, which I can't get from introspection or reflection on my feelings or analyzing my sensations. These are questions about a word's meaning.

Now most of us don't assess and analyze a conversation as it actually takes place simply because we have 2P knowledge that we have learned over time — knowledge about human interactions. We do the same thing when it comes to reading Shakespeare or the Bible. Since these are different thought worlds with different languages, we have a discipline called hermeneutics, which is another kind of 2P knowledge to help us understand what other people put into print.

When I include you in the mix of my thoughts and in my world, the circle gets bigger and now includes something outside of myself. Once I include you, I have to rely on something quite different from 1P knowledge. When you enter my world, issues of how to treat you arise. What is kindness or meanness? How should I deal with you in business or when we have a dispute?—these are issues that fall into the category of ethics. This is unique 2P knowledge. As long as I'm thinking only about my internal thoughts and feelings and doing the work of introspection, the issue of ethics never arises. But as soon as I talk to you, or as soon as you are present, you and I are now "we"—and how "we" are going to relate to each other is something "we" will decide. This is 2P knowledge.

3P: Knowledge I have about abstract stuff out there—physics, chemistry, biology, for example—is 3P knowledge, third person "out there" knowledge. For instance, I know that a water molecule is made up of two hydrogen atoms and one oxygen. This is 3P knowledge. I didn't talk to water to find that out; I studied water in high school chemistry to learn that fact. I didn't get this knowledge from personal introspection (1P) or from analysis about you and me and how we are going to relate (2P); I got it from empirical observations "out there" (3P).

Subjective versus Objective

Perhaps you can see how this discussion of 1P, 2P, and 3P understandings of God fits into the Greek categories of truth, beauty, and goodness. Traditionally, truth is thought of as whatever comes through the five senses and can be tested. In other words, science has been the tool to get at the domain of truth, and this has often been referred to as "objective" truth. This is the domain of 3P knowledge.

Beauty can't be tested or verified. The old saying "Beauty is in the eye of the beholder" reveals that beauty is 1P knowledge. What I think is beautiful may not be what you think is even remotely close to beautiful. When we are talking about this "personal taste" sort of truth, it is often referred to as "subjective."

The word *subjective* is often used in tones that conclude that it is an inferior sort of knowledge when compared to objective knowledge. In reality, though, 3P and 1P knowledge aren't inferior or superior to each other; they are simply different kinds of knowledge. I can't overemphasize how many disputes about the existence of God and religious experience evaporate when we realize that there are different kinds of knowledge and therefore different tools for coming to know within these varying types.

When we talk about *goodness* or *the good*, we are talking about ethics. This is the domain of 2P knowledge. When I include another person into the context of relating, we are in a 2P situation. This isn't objective or subjective knowledge but interpersonal or intersubjective knowledge.[1]

A New Playing Field for Knowing

Let's reflect a bit on what has happened with these sorts of knowledge. Up to the time of the Enlightenment, when rationalism took over, Western society had a high regard for the place that spiritual knowledge could play in a person's life and even in public discourse. No one thought someone loony if he or she felt certain spiritual premonitions, had dreams they took seriously, or simply used a lot of "god talk." In other words, 1P knowledge — interior, spiritual language — was accepted, and you might say even expected. This interior knowledge wasn't considered inferior; in fact, in certain historical periods it might have been considered the starting point and even the most important kind of knowledge because this is where spiritual knowledge is to be found.[2] Not only was this sort of 1P knowledge valuable; there was a definite recognition that this sort of knowing wasn't simply "head knowing." There was a sense you could know things in physical or embodied ways.

Cultural historian Morris Berman has made a strong case that in eras gone by we had strong *somatic* knowledge; that is, our bodies registered when we sensed danger, had a "gut feeling," sensed that "something just wasn't right." These were types of knowing not associated with the mind but held in equally high regard in previous eras. He argues that our inability to pay attention to our, quite literally, full-bodied knowledge transmitters has led us to being a culture that is impoverished and numb to the deep visceral wiring in our very design.[3] Is this is one of the reasons most of us have to be taught (often late in life) that intuition, usually experienced through some somatic sensation, is something to be valued? Is this why our extremely reliable intuition is a foreign category of knowing for most people throughout most of life?[4]

With the rise of rationalism and the Enlightenment, a dramatic shift happens. Subjective knowledge (1P) is placed on the back burner as something far too personal to be reliable, and in its place comes the new knowledge darling—science. In the scientific world, hypothesis, evidence, and verification take center stage (3P). If it can't be proved, it is suspect and certainly can't be too reliable. Science with its tools of telescopes, microscopes, beakers, flames, and test tubes will prove and verify what is legitimate. What can't stand up to this scrutiny is considered inferior and unreliable. How can science, specifically designed with tools for 3P knowledge, ever tap, mine, explore, or do experiments on 1P knowledge that is resident in an entirely different world called the mind, the heart, internal experience? You can sense the dilemma. There aren't only different kinds of knowledge; there are different tools to get at these different types of knowledge.

Knowledge Shift

Enough with the quick history lesson. Can you see where this is going? Can you see how this has affected our work in the area of spiritual conversations? Can you see why things over the last fifteen to twenty years have genuinely undergone a transition? Let's do a brief cultural summary of the modern world and the shift toward this new world called *postmodern.*

The modern world of science (3P knowledge) has reigned supreme, and the advances in this arena prove it. Scientific and technological advances in medicine, computers and computation, robotics, nanotechnology, and mapping of the human genome (the result of a confluence of biology and computer/computational advances) prove beyond the shadow of a doubt that the last thirty to fifty years are the fullest flowering to date of the age of rationalism.[5]

For all the advances however, many people have noted that our ethics and morals (2P knowledge) have seemingly not kept developmental pace with our 3P scientific advancements. Two atom bombs in the twentieth century, chemical warfare, gas chambers, and a world ecosystem literally coming apart lead most people to conclude we haven't managed to mature our interactions with other humans and our planet nearly as much as we have our 3P knowledge.

Knowledge about science and technology soars, but 2P knowledge—how this should be used to create a better world—hasn't developed as quickly. This is exactly why the big questions of what constitutes being a person (big conversation in reproductive technologies and stem cell research), when does life begin, when does life end (euthanasia conversation), all fall in the 2P area, while 3P scientific knowledge marches on unchecked. Let's reflect on the reason this has happened.

Scientific knowledge development is impersonal; by definition it is "it." When you are working on "it," you don't have to simultaneously worry about the application of the "it" technology being developed—someone else can do that. It is in part why we have had to recently develop these things called "hospital ethics committees." Ethics Committees are 2P organisms developed to ensure that 3P knowledge and technology isn't used to harm people. The field of bioethics, relatively unknown just three or four decades ago, is now a discipline all its own. Now 2P knowledge is trying to catch up with 3P advances.

New Apologetics

Can we translate this into our spiritual conversation area? What is the point of all this historical and cultural reflection? It has much to do with what is permissible within public conversation and why we need a new apologetics (see also our discussion in chapter 7).

Let's make sure we understand what we mean by the word *apologetics*. Apologetics has traditionally been the discipline for providing rational reasons for why we believe what we believe about God, Jesus, and the Bible. Apologetics helps us realize that our faith is grounded in something more than thin air, that there are good reasons for us to believe the things we believe. Apologetics has often been applied a bit more broadly as well—not just a mound of evidence to help us ground our faith but a tool to prove to those outside of faith there are good reasons to give faith a try. This idea is rooted in 1 Peter 3:15, where the Greek word *apologia* is translated "reason." So how does apologetics fare these days?

In a modern rationalist, scientific world where 3P knowledge is supreme and 1P knowledge is suspect, having conversations about spiritual things is zany, a non sequitur, and a throwback to a less enlightened age. Thus most modern people, or people born and bred in the modern era, are a little skeptical about spiritual things.

But some interesting things have happened in science that show our physical world and invisible spiritual world may be far more connected than originally thought. Is it possible that these discoveries showing the deep interconnectedness of our world has given people the permission to explore and discuss the longings and yearnings deep inside them? Great scientific advancement and technological progress cannot provide answers or satisfy the deep-seated human yearnings. Accelerating amounts of 3P knowledge simply can't do it — and never will.

Rationalist apologetics has fallen on hard times these days. Evidentialist apologetics, birthed largely in the 1970s, was right in line with the modernist scientific world's approach.[6] The evangelical establishment either decided to play by the rules of the modern world or were unknowingly co-opted by the spirit of the age and are now relegated to the margins because of it. In any case, the passing of an era and the emergence of another is an opportunity to learn from the past and to become more effective in the future.

With the dying of the modern world and the questioning of the supremacy of 3P knowledge, a new dynamic has emerged in our landscape. It's almost as if all the 3P knowledge pursuits, as good and helpful as they have been, have created an aridity and desolateness in the human spirit that cry out to be quenched. In the postmodern world, where 3P knowledge is valued along with the more personal and subjective 1P knowledge, there is a fresh admission that we need more than hard-core science.[7] We need a world where technological advance (3P) is framed by equally important considerations of how these advances affect human lives and the ecosystem (2P). Some of those insights may come from people who understand the vast, millenniums-old traditions of introspection and reflection on spiritual things and how these practices should inform and frame our decisions and directions (1P).[8]

In the arena of apologetics we need something far more relational and internal if we are going to see people, who have deeply interior longings, truly satisfied. Do you catch the shift I'm suggesting? We Christians have spent our apologetics horsepower on 3P evidence building; but proof that the resurrection was a real, historical event, which is impossible to prove, is not the right starting point for spiritual conversations these days. We must consider a personal, intimate starting point — a 1P starting point.

Remember that 1P knowledge is deeply personal — no one can talk you out of it. I think that if we develop a deeply relational apologetics (2P) that taps into the deep core yearnings of people's hearts (1P), we will never see a need for rationalist apologetics (3P) in our postmodern world.

CHAPTER 10

Yearnings for Wholeness

"I would just love to be whole! I hate feeling so broken and shattered. There has to be something out there that can heal my hurt. I go to church. I do what I am supposed to—but the life I'm getting in return doesn't seem to be this 'peace thing' everyone talks about. How many more hoops do I have to jump through before God will give me a break?"

Yes, Ethan is expressing some anger, and no, he doesn't have the full view. But this was his rant the first time he came to a Learning Community meeting on a Thursday night. He was frustrated and spent. What he did note, however, was that shalom and wholeness were things he assumed were attainable and available. No matter how difficult things were for him, he just knew there was a possibility that something better existed.

What if being made *imago dei* is God's architectural design that drives our desire for the very things God provided in the garden of Eden? And while we're on the topic, we should ask just what it was that God provided in the garden. At the core of God's architectural design of our spirit, there seem to be yearnings that drive our quest—yearnings for transformation, to be something more, to be defined by something bigger.

A Desire for Wholeness

Every human being seems to think that wholeness is desirable and attainable. In fact, in our culture of narcissism, to use Christopher Lasch's term, some say they are entitled to and deserve wholeness.[1] This default setting seems to be universal and cross-cultural —pointing to a wiring, so to speak, a "built into the human psyche" expectation. It is God's transformational architecture designed into the very breath breathed into every human being. I wonder if this expectation isn't, in fact, a clue to something that is deeply connected to our origins, a hint of our primal yearnings and intentional design. According to Genesis, we were made for the garden.

Is the universal primal desire for the environment of the garden part of what is inherent in the *imago dei*? It is important to remember that when the Israelites were in exile, two of their prophets noted that the nation's ultimate longing was to return to Eden, a restoration to the original shalom and provision of the garden.[2]

Is it possible that the only thing every human being throughout all of history has shared is the desire to return to the garden? Clearly this isn't how everyone may articulate it, but when the garden is defined as a place of plush, provisioned protection, a place of wholeness and wellness, a place where happiness—true happiness—is reality, then this longing does indeed seem universal. And if the answer is, "Yes, we do have this shared desire," then we are hovering over a very important observation: Something inherent in the *imago dei*, in every human being, creates a longing for garden conditions. We humans have a built-in yearning to return to, or at least to make an attempt to replicate, garden conditions.

While we all may long for garden conditions—shalom wellness and wholeness—it is our human attempt to replicate garden conditions that gets us into trouble. This is the trajectory on which spiritual conversations can travel. To that issue we will have to return as we look at the human foibles and failings in trying to reproduce the garden environment. Our track record shows that, try as we may, we fall short in our efforts to rebuild a garden setting and end up creating an inferior and often dysfunctional and addictive substitute.

While we all have a longing for wholeness, I want to be quick to acknowledge that this shalom completeness can be experienced differently or defined uniquely, depending on context. The definition of shalom may have common core dimensions, but what wholeness looked and felt like to the paralyzed man in Mark 2, for example, may have been quite different from what it meant to the woman at the well in John 4. What wholeness looked like to a man with leprosy or to a woman subject to bleeding or to Jairus, whose daughter had died, varied for each and was quite situational. What shalom means to my next-door neighbor is likely quite different from what it means to my sixteen-year-old's best friend. While there may be core similarities, the surrounding dimensions may connect in more thematic than specific ways. This reality doesn't undermine the idea of a universal shalom inherent in the *imago dei*; it simply recognizes that there are contextual dimension to the details of how shalom unfolds throughout various times and cultural locations. Wholeness at some level has subjective and highly personalized dimensions, but there is some sense in which we all seek wholeness and wellness.

This seeking of wholeness or wellness is what I'm calling a fundamental core yearning—a yearning that is part of the transformational architecture with which God has designed every human.

Eternity in the Human Heart

How, then, does this architecture make itself known? What does a new starting point for a new conversation mean in practical terms? What implications will it have on how our lives are shaped and reshaped as narrative? It means we begin to hover over, listen for, draw out, and ask questions around the core yearnings that emerge out of *imago dei*. A return to the garden is in order, but we will do it via a side trip in Ecclesiastes as we learn from the wisdom of Solomon.

Christians can't be in a church long before hearing an Old Testament sermon on "the God-shaped hole in our hearts." The language is nearly a brand in conservative circles for the eternal longing that God has placed in every human heart. The Old Testament text used as the basis for this idea comes from Solomon's words in Ecclesiastes:

> What do workers gain from their toil? I have seen the burden God has laid on the human race. He has made everything beautiful in its time. He has also set eternity in the human heart; yet no one can fathom what God has done from beginning to end. I know that there is nothing better for people than to be happy and to do good while they live. That each of them may eat and drink, and find satisfaction in all their toil—this is the gift of God. I know that everything God does will endure forever; nothing can be added to it and nothing taken from it. God does it so that people will fear him.
>
> Ecclesiastes 3:9–14

Plenty of brilliant commentators have written about Ecclesiastes, so I will dispense with framing this particular text. The gist of the book is that life is futile if all we do is get caught up in the routines of life with no thought of anything further. Solomon further challenges the idea that our lives will be fuller by filling them with more money, power, prestige, or beauty. All of these, he says, are a foolish "chasing after the wind." He is quick to point out that there is an interior architectural design housing some deep yearnings that are seeking expression. Solomon calls the architecture "eternity in the human heart." Something deep in the human spirit seeks, quests, longs for, and looks for something more than the mundane routines of life — or at least something that can energize and bring meaning to the routines and even ruts of everyday existence.

The question is, "How does this eternity in our hearts express itself? How does this eternity in our hearts become visible — and if it becomes visible, is there a way to converse about it?" If our reading of Ecclesiastes is right, then a part of our designed interior architecture is this drive for transformation into a state and place of shalom. We would then be brought to an important place for spiritual conversation — and note, it is very much a 1P sort of knowledge: subjective, personal, and interior.

I think when we get in touch with three core connections and yearnings — and even their infected counterparts — we are hovering over the place of greatest gravity when it comes to spiritual conversations. These built-in transformation seekers automatically surface in the life of every human being. If other people have these built-in yearnings and drives, why wouldn't we learn to listen for them and become aware of those times when we are being presented with opportunities for meaningful conversations?

Core Connections and Yearnings

In reflecting on the things God placed in the garden for Adam and Eve, I want to expand on the concept I introduced in chapter 1 with regard to the Latin word *cultus* (from *colere*, which translates the English "to care"). Combining the first four letters (*cult*—don't think religious cult, cult leader, or cult following) with various word endings yields helpful reminders of the garden.

Presumably God created Adam and Eve not because he had to but because he wanted to. It isn't a stretch to realize that God, while not needing to create human beings, put in place the possibility of relationship with his creation. In the Old Testament, the Israelites carried out their relationship with God through the sacrificial *cultus*. This system was the way in which the people of God lived within the framework of the "family rules" and showed their care for and connection to God. There seems to be no doubt that Adam and Eve were made with this *vertical connection* as part of their very design. Just as a baby bonds to her parents and knows their voices and touch, so too Adam and Eve knew God and his voice and touch. The *cultus connection* to God is garden-given and inherent in the human architecture.

A second architectural detail to our design also seems inescapable. After a litany of "it was good" in the opening chapter of Genesis, God did find something that was not good—it was "not good for the man to be alone."[3] Relationship this time isn't vertical with God but horizontal with each other. We might use the word *culture* as shorthand for this second relationship. Adam and Eve were to find complementarity in the other. Adam found a completeness with Eve that was absent without her. Culture is how our relationships with each other and the artifacts around us function. The *culture connection* to each other is garden-given as well.

A third relationship for Adam and Eve exists—one expressly and specifically given by God. They are given a relationship with the dirt. They are to *cultivate* the garden. While some may want to make this relationship exclusively about the ecology issue, this dirt connection points to something else. Adam and Eve's commissioning to cultivate the world around them seems to be a broad metaphor for their sense of purpose and destiny. Exactly in this sense of destiny are the seeds of hope. The ability to make an impact on tomorrow, to contribute to—though not control—the future, and to shape and mold the trajectory of their existence is the core of hope. They were to be keeping the soil, tending the earth, and watching over the creation that God had entrusted them with. They were cultivating the earth—and in so doing they were cultivating and shaping their tomorrow. Adam and Eve were given purpose, destiny, and hope in the cultivating project. This *cultivation connection* to the dirt is the third garden-given yearning.

These three relationships—with God, with each other, and with the dirt—summarize in a holistic way what God created in the opening scene of the Genesis story.

What if *cultus* (connection to the divine), *culture* (connection to others), and *cultivation* (connection to a God-designed purpose and destiny) are the primary architectural building blocks of *imago dei*? These three components designed by our Creator inspire and motivate our behavior. Furthermore this architecture, this software coding, is expressly designed to seek or crave an upgrade—a software patch that makes the whole thing finally work right. What if our goal in spiritual conversations is simply to point people in the right direction as those yearnings come to the surface?

God's mandate to Adam and Eve to benevolently and creatively interact with and oversee, serve, rule, and provide leadership to the creation is a prototype of the human experience. Adam and Eve have a built-in motivation to care about the dirt around them, to mold and shape their tomorrow by shaping the creation both with their words by naming things and with their hands by cultivating things. This is their purpose and destiny. Every human being's purpose may be shaped differently, but the quest for a sense of purpose is part of our interior architecture.

Our hearts also seem designed to deeply connect in relationship with other people—to love and be loved, to celebrate and be celebrated. What if we are wired to crave and yearn for unconditional love and acceptance?

I think we realize that the quest to find God isn't a crutch for weak people or a figment of the human imagination but is actually part of our interior architecture. What if the yearning to define ourselves by something bigger than our own skin is part of the seeds that sprout into full-blown life change and transformation?

Digging Deeper into the Core Yearnings

I have already mentioned my wonderings about these core yearnings being rooted in the *imago dei* back in the garden. So let's take a deeper look and see what emerges. We'll begin by looking at the God-ward dimension.

The Yearning to Believe

The potency of this God-ward connection is hard to overestimate. Adam and Eve are given a relationship with God that invades their consciousness and defines who they are. Can you imagine carrying around with you for an entire lifetime the clear sense that you had been handmade by God? No matter what came your way, no matter what problems you encountered, no matter how dark the struggles, it would be hard to escape the fact that you had been made by God and commissioned to be his representative for the world to see. This would be a story you would tell yourself over and over again—a story that would have a powerful impact on your sense of worth, value, and place in God's world.

God made Adam and Eve in his image and gave them the capacity and charge to rule/serve and to lovingly and selflessly act on his behalf as his representatives. Adam and Eve are given the opportunity to sense a transcendence and a connection to something bigger than themselves. As God's representatives made in God's image and charged with keeping the created order intact, they are created as inherently valuable. They are different from birds, fish, and trees. They are granted meaning and purpose, which is woven into the core of their very being.

I find this observation fascinating, not because it is so profound, but because a sense of "we must be here for some reason" and "there must be something more out there than simply me and we" is so universal. The core yearning to uncover a sense of meaning and purpose seems to know no ethnic, continental, or time boundaries—this yearning is not confined to one epoch in global history. The sense that there must be some meaning and purpose in life and that it must be related to some "power out there bigger than me" seems so intuitive that it hardly needs mentioning.

When we look back at philosophies such as atheistic existentialism or nihilism—philosophies that undercut any sense of purpose or meaning in life—we find that they are doomed to fail. And there's a good reason. No one can indefinitely sustain the opposite of life having meaning and purpose. Listen to people talk. They operate with underlying, tacit, and unproved assumptions:

"There must be a reason for being. There must be something more than just my life of seventy to eighty years. There must be something that breathes a sense of destiny into the fabric of human existence — because if that's not the case, the world is nothing but an elaborate fluky accident."

Most of this *is* tacit; most of it *is* unconscious. I've had the opportunity to facilitate a number of "discover your mission in life" seminars. What drives hundreds of people to these events is their assumption there must be some purpose to their life. If they didn't believe that, they wouldn't be at a seminar that promised to equip them to write a mission statement in the next thirty days. People come to these events for a second reason. They usually have no idea what their purpose is or have only a vague sense of it. Where did they come up with the idea that life has purpose? I suggest that it is resident within *imago dei*. I don't think a lot of people probe the history of philosophy, plumbing the depths for answers to the question of why they exist. But talk to people, listen to them, watch movies, read novels — you will see evidence of this universal assumption: life must have meaning.

Anthropologist Ellen Dissanayake notes that humans seem to have a reflexive desire to artistically make the places they live "their own." She observes that from the cardboard box huts painted with stain made from crushed berries in Brazil to the decorating of a fire pit by a single mother in a thatched hut in an African tribal community to piercing and tattooing of the body, the universal experience is that we want to express ourselves through art.[4]

Her conclusion that art is at its essence "making special" is instructive for us. In art we are placing a mark on something that individualizes it, customizes it with our thumbprint, makes it something uniquely our own. The ability to "make special" is rooted in our connection to God and his charge to creatively and lovingly serve the world. The New Testament picks up on this idea and declares that we are "God's handiwork."[5] We are God's art piece, his painting, his sculpture—or, as Jeremiah puts it, a "pot" shaped from the clay—God's pottery piece.[6] If the essence of art is making special—making unique—then our ability to make special is rooted in the fact that *we have been made special.* Any and all interest and ability to do so is derivative.

What does this mean for spiritual conversation? Quite a bit, actually. I wonder if every time we hear someone make statements about purpose or express hidden assumptions about it, we are not in fact hovering over one of God's architectural design elements—a core yearning that is really nothing but a reflection of, or one expression of, the eternity set in the human heart and expressed by the quest to believe that I am here for a reason, that I exist for something more than simply propagating the human race. I think the craving to believe that "life is more than what I see" is one of the incontrovertible and universal dimensions of human experience. The interest in creating and making special is nothing but a carrying out of the mandate given to Adam and Eve, an unmistakable echo of a divine imprint on our lives.

When we look at human history, the default expression of nearly every people group around the globe and throughout every time period has been that there must be something more out there. This default expression—whether through constructing totem poles, worshiping the sun god, or believing in the Trinitarian God of Christian theology—is existent and pervasive. And this built-in core yearning or craving is not the result of empirical research, hypothesis, and evidential research. It is wholly intuitive and internal. It is 1P knowledge that has little or no connection at all to the tools and sensibilities of 3P scientific knowledge. And we don't just have history to support this idea.

The next time you're in a conversation with someone and she begins to talk as if life—not life in general but *her life*—has a purpose, a sense of destiny, ask her why she believes that. Don't provide answers or your opinion; just say something like, "I'm curious about your sense that life has meaning. Where does that come from? I've always been interested in that myself." Another one I love is, "I notice you talk as if your life has some sort of goal or purpose. Have you ever reflected on where that comes from, or is it just an assumption you operate with?"

You can certainly have interesting conversations about these deeply rooted assumptions, but the conversation becomes even more revealing when you challenge the universal sense that "we must have some sort of meaning and purpose in our lives"—saying things like, "I notice you assume that life has some sort of meaning or destiny to it. Why not assume exactly the opposite, that life is a bad joke and it really has no purpose or goal and there really is no reason we are here?" Unless you've dialogued with people along these lines before, you may be surprised at how that counterintuitive question strikes most people. I have yet to find one person I've engaged in conversation who hasn't pushed back strongly on this question. They assume, tacitly but strongly nonetheless, that there must be some sort of purpose to their existence.

You may be thinking that not *every single person* expresses this "universal craving." I acknowledge that there are some diehard nihilists out there who do seem to think that all of life is meaningless and pointless. But without getting into the details of it all, they don't tend to live out that belief consistently. If all of life is meaningless because there is no God (because if there is a God, there must be some reason he made all this), then there is also no way to distinguish good from bad in any kind of binding way. Everything becomes opinion and perspective. When that happens, if I choose to treat you badly, you might cry foul that I am being nasty, but you would have no moral ground or binding ethical reason for doing so. When there is no God, there are only arbitrary values.

The Yearning to Belong

Adam's aloneness was the first thing in the garden not pronounced as "good." Aloneness is not how we are dominantly wired. Our architectural design called for something different right from the start. In fact, solitary confinement is used as the harshest form of imprisonment. Being alone for a brief period may be a part of the rhythm many of us crave and need to be healthy; aloneness all the time, however, is simply not healthy. In fact, all of life is a constant battle between the with-ness attraction and the aloneness attraction. We want to be with others but not get swallowed up by them. We also want to be alone and individual but not to the degree that we are isolated and become an island unto ourselves.

These thoughts on with-ness and aloneness are the foundation of the family systems theory of psychiatrist Murray Bowen. Here's how one of his protégés puts it: "One of the most fundamental features of the human condition is the struggle that arises out of the need to strike a balance between two basic urges: the drive toward being an individual—one alone, autonomous—and the drive toward being together with others in relationship. Ideally these two tendencies are brought into a fulfilling balance. More often, however, the result is an unremitting tension."[7]

We have been wired for interdependent healthy community.[8] And while there are a lot of things we may be seeking when we are in community, underneath all drives for community is the need for unconditional love and acceptance. It was not good for Adam to be alone because our development as humans is deeply intertwined with the most maturing force known to human-ity—love.[9] The *cult*- word we used here was *culture*. God created a culture of mutuality, of working together, of loving, of caring, and of doing life together. God expects—and has built in to the fabric of life—that we will play together, laugh together, learn together, and come to know together.

This sense of deep longing to belong is inescapable; yet in our Western world of isolated individualism we aren't sure how to relate well to others. Is it any wonder that most of the biblical passages that encourage us to specific behaviors are usually interpreted by us as individual challenges we should apply in our personal life, even though many are actually charges to the whole community and are assumed to be worked out in the context of us-ness, or community?[10] It is impossible to miss the importance of unconditional love and acceptance, whether you're talking about how important it is for newborns to be loved and touched and held, or about teenagers who, when alienated, often head down destructive paths, even toward suicide.

When we begin talking to people and listening to them, we realize that their hurts, pains, and disappointments often (though not always) have to do with a lack of unconditional love and ac-ceptance. When there is lack of love, the pain is nearly universal. It cuts through cultures and eras of time, and across ethnic bound-aries. When people head into conversations about unconditional love, they are once more hovering over *imago dei* themes that put us right at the core of our design.

We have a core yearning to connect with at least one other person who will unconditionally love and accept us, warts and all.

Why the drive? Why the core yearning? What is it that makes us think we should be recipients of love? Why is it so central to our development as humans? Why is it the fundamental descriptor of God?[11] Why is so much of our significance and self-understanding tied up in whether or not we are unconditionally loved? These questions and conversations put us into another arena of spiritual conversations. I wonder if it has to do with *imago dei*.

How many times do we hear friends, family members, or spouses say, "Why can't you just accept me the way I am? Why can't you just love me as is? Why do you have to constantly try to change me?" What is behind questions like these? Isn't there a built-in assumption that somehow, someway, a divine favor out there entitles us to this kind of love? That's wild! It is built into our very architecture.

As I suggested with another built-in assumption — that life must have meaning — try counterquestioning on this issue of unconditional love too. Whenever anyone asks why can't they just be loved and accepted as is, they are appealing to some invisible law or rule or universal vibe out there that they are assuming everyone somehow subscribes to, correct? What do you think would happen if we were to suggest just the opposite — that in fact we actually *shouldn't* accept and love people unconditionally, that we should only offer love with full expectation of reciprocity?

No. Hold it. What if we offer love only after we have first been loved? What if we act on the basis of a belief that love should work on totally selfish grounds and all this hoopla of selfless unconditionality is a mythic vestige of some previous religious era and we need to get on with the "eye for an eye" model of loving?

Certainly some already live their lives this way; but these very same people will very likely tell you that they are entitled to this unconditionality and acceptance. In other words, they acknowledge that there *is* some sort of unwritten code out there to which they are appealing.

Note the connection between the first core yearning—to believe something about our purpose or unique design, about why we are here—and this second core yearning of unconditional love and acceptance. These two pieces, placed together, have an interesting interplay beyond just the family systems observations made earlier.

The Hungarian-born Mihaly Csikszentmihalyi is a researcher and author in the area of creativity and personal flow. He has made interesting observations about how we define happiness in our lives. After hundreds of interviews and years of research, he has concluded that there are two primary elements comprising what we associate with happiness. One is what he calls the process of *differentiation*, which involves the recognition of our unique contribution to the world, our unique wiring, our expression of our being in action. The second process involves what he calls *integration*, which is the realization that while we are unique, we are also "completely enmeshed in networks of relationships with other human beings, with cultural symbols and artifacts, and with the surrounding natural environment."[12] He claims that our total fulfillment of our potentialities on both of these fronts is the basis of happiness. The person who is both fully integrated and fully differentiated is what he calls a "complex individual" and has the best chance of leading a healthy and meaningful life.[13]

I find it helpful to recognize that cutting-edge research corroborates what we have discovered from our reflections on *imago dei* and the core yearnings associated with it. Why is this a helpful tool? If two of the three core yearnings rooted in *imago dei* are the fundamental components leading researchers tell us make for healthy, well-adjusted human beings, then we can have some very interesting starting points in research that enable us to move the conversation to the issue of the way we have been created.

I think it is the quest for happiness (usually carried on in inappropriate ways) in an effort to get back to the garden that gives us all sorts of grist for the conversation mill. This is a hint that we'll need to move on in our conversations to talk about the infection we have contracted and the impact it has on our architectural design.

The Yearning to Become

One other element grounded in the *imago dei* places us in a unique spot in the grand scheme of creation. When God granted Adam and Eve, and therefore all of humanity, with creative ability, design ability, architectural, civil, and artistic ability, God was granting them the opportunity to envision a tomorrow that holds within it the possibility of being different from today. This seems to be a uniquely human trait. I am not thinking that deer or polar bears or hummingbirds have this sort of built-in future homing mechanism. They certainly have instincts about what to do as the future momentarily unfolds, but this expectation of a preferable tomorrow seems exclusively human. The word we use for this connection to a better tomorrow is *hope*.

When you take a look at how all human beings envision the future, you will again find a universal phenomenon: we have an innate ability to expect and assume that tomorrow will be at least as good as today, and we have a full expectation that it may in fact improve. We make the assumption that tomorrow will be a better tomorrow. We talk as if it is true, work to make it happen, assume that everyone else wants it too, and generally live from the default setting that it is a natural drive.

Mihaly Csikszentmihalyi weighs in again on this issue, claiming that human beings cannot survive without hope. He argues that *apart from hope*, what I'm calling the ability to create or enter a preferable tomorrow, human beings are reduced to an animal existence where biology reigns.[14]

Csikszentmihalyi notes that in former times the brokers of this sort of hope were clergy; they were the voices who had preeminence and were sought out to make sense of it all. His conclusion is that those days are gone, and science coupled with smart business practices is the best route to a world filled with hope.[15] I've had to wonder if I've abdicated my responsibility to be a hope bringer. Are people looking elsewhere for hope because in my life and ministry I am not consciously making known the very essence of the grand story of God?

This is obviously profoundly sad and deeply dissatisfying. Those of us entrusted with the insights about the treasures of *imago dei* and the forum for communicating its riches — the church — have gone soft, reduced the message to religious mumbo jumbo, and have gotten out of the hope business to the point that a leading researcher at the University of Chicago says we need to look now to good business and science. Ouch! Yet he is quick to admit that most business leaders aren't too excited to broker meaning, much less joy and hope.

Hope says we can make a difference. And since the infection of Adam and Eve with selfishness, hope of a better or different tomorrow becomes even more important. Hope says we aren't the victims of a horrible fate set in motion and incapable of being stopped. Hope says the possibility, even probability, of a better tomorrow isn't a pipe dream. Hope says it doesn't matter how bad today is and how beat-up you feel, tomorrow won't be as bad. All of this hope stuff is innately human; it is all rooted in *imago dei*.

In fact, most people recognize the absence of such hope as something pathological, something that can even lead to the ultimate despair—to the desire to end one's life, to suicide.

When we are hovering over hope for a better tomorrow, we are honing in on *imago dei*. Hope is built-in. When we move from a fall-redemption summary to a creation-fall-redemption-restoration summary of the story, hope is what directs us toward the restoration; and the *imago dei* and garden piece of the story in creation is what gives us a sense of what we are trying to be restored to. Without the garden and a clear sense of God's purpose there, we would have no idea what the restoration project is all about and why Jesus even came.

These three yearnings when taken together seem to approximate what a shalom wholeness would look like. What could possibly be more whole or life-giving than living in a condition in which your awareness of a connection to God and of being made by him (and therefore being part of something bigger than yourself) is coupled with an experience of community in which you get to join others who have the same sense you do and to cocreate with God and serve the world in ways that instill hope in you and the others around you? This seems to be a great description of shalom, wholeness, and wellness.

We now have a better understanding of what we are trying to see happen in the arena of spiritual conversations. Listen for core yearnings; probe, question, and note the often blind spot assumptions people have concerning these cravings that are deep in their hearts. Draw out the "why" of these yearnings. Why are they there? Why do people make these sorts of assumptions? Why don't they make the opposite assumptions and hold them just as reflexively and intuitively? As those organic conversations transpire, we have to be aware of the various ways in which God enters into the language and ideas being discussed. If we only listen for 2P language, then we're missing a couple of other potential gold mines of possibility. 1P and 3P language also reveal a "God openness." Our hope is to meet people where they are, to grapple with their understandings of their yearnings to connect to the divine and how all of this is playing out in their lives.

Infection: Yearnings Careening Off Course

If these are the core yearnings deep within every human spirit, then why can't we all just get along? What is so complicated? Why don't things work out? Shouldn't everyone just follow those yearnings and see everything turn out OK? If the software is in place, if the architectural design is solid, what is the problem? What happened?

Adam and Eve, who had been entrusted with lovingly, creatively, and selflessly serving the world, and thereby being God's image and representation on the planet, were tempted. Eve's and Adam's eating the fruit from the tree of the knowledge of good and evil changed everything. From this point forward in the story, something shifts. This virus, this infection, changes all the relationships established in the garden: God-ward (*cultus*—connection to the divine), human-ward (*culture*—connection to each other), and dirt-ward (*cultivate*—connection to the earth as their purpose). An infection took hold that made every one of those relationships unhealthy. From this point forward, we see every yearning infected—the mandate given to Adam and Eve to benevolently and creatively interact with and oversee the world, to be the image and representatives of God, to be his likeness in the new land he had just designed. We see benevolence shift to malevolence. From this point on, we see loving creativity and service toward each other and the garden/world infected and polluted.

The tragedy of the Adam and Eve infection is a move from selflessness to selfishness. They were to have acted as God would act — to be his representatives, his presence, his hands, his feet, his image and likeness. But they are now infected with a virus that constantly taints them with self-interest. From this time forward, the Genesis narrative is marked by selfish act after selfish act.

What is important for our conversation is that this selfishness is what ultimately gets Adam and Eve kicked out of the garden — an expulsion that is highly symbolic. For with their move from the garden, the three characteristics summarized in our *cult*-words — *cultus, culture, cultivate* — take a huge beating. At the same time, the core architecture of our spirit, which is connected to these words, is now polluted and perverted. To complicate matters further, we are now displaced from the place where our deepest longings could be satisfied. Did you hear that? The move from the garden is a move from the place that was custom-designed to fulfill the core yearnings inherent in the *imago dei*.

The move from the garden is a clear indication that Adam and Eve are being removed from the presence of God. Obviously the God-ward cultus connection is damaged. But the move from the garden also clearly marks a damaging of the culture — the relational connection of Adam and Eve. When we read about the ramifications of the fall in Genesis 3:14–19, it is obvious that their relationship will be strained, and all relationships from that time forward will feel the same strain. What's more, the cultivated, dirt-ward dimension is marred. We are told that the land has been infected too ("Cursed is the ground because of you").[16] In other words, the three primary relationships Adam and Eve have — with

God, each other, and the earth—are fractured. And while it isn't directly stated in the text, it is clear that the relationship with self was also affected. The first emotion Adam and Eve experienced after the serpent event was shame—shame about something that had existed from the time they were brought to life, namely, their nakedness. When they ate from the tree, something inside of them was broken, and their interior world was infected and fractured. Their experience of their own inner space would never be the same.

Garden Yearnings Outside the Garden

Here is the challenge for the arena of spiritual conversations. The three architectural elements built into us—summarized as "eternity in the human heart"—and experienced as the yearning to believe there is something bigger than ourselves, the yearning to belong in community and experience unconditional love and acceptance, and the yearning to become, fueling a hope of something new and vigorous awaiting us in the future, are now placed outside the garden, which was the primary place for the fulfillment of these yearnings.

We were built with garden yearnings, but we moved away from the place designed to fulfill them. So what does humanity do? We set out on our own quest to fulfill these garden yearnings. Did you hear that? *This is a central piece to this whole spiritual conversation thing: humanity is on a quest to get these garden yearnings fulfilled.* They, of course, may not know it has to do with these "garden yearnings," but they are familiar with the drive inside, the gap inside, the chasm, the hunger, the hollowness.

God designed human beings with these core yearnings. They are in the very software architecture of our spirit. But part of the problem now encountered is what to do with these drives when the location they are designed for is now a foreign land.

Welcome to the human condition. We are deeply infected with a selfishness that causes us to attempt to satisfy the core yearnings in ways they cannot be satisfied—because outside of the relationships of the garden, all that exists are cheap, hollow, thin, addictive, though sometimes exhilarating, alternatives. To attempt to live out these substitutes is to rewrite our personal narratives in ways that are bound to have dissatisfying endings.

This is what we need to watch for. Core yearnings when moved from the relationship of the garden become ferocious appetites that can lead to addictive behaviors and damaging patterns. Let's take a brief look at how core yearnings have careened off course and have us heading for a ditch.

To Believe

The core yearning to believe—to believe something about why we are here, what our purpose is, whether we have anything to contribute to this world, to be connected to something bigger than ourselves—when not developed within a garden relationship with the Garden Maker leads to what? Drive for power, prestige, title, corporate accolades, peer strokes, and lots of other things we would like to define ourselves by. Do you see what is at stake in all this? When we are made *imago dei*—and know that to be the case—we can walk with a sense of self-definition and self-understanding that connects us to the Creator of the universe who has invited us to be his representatives on the planet. But remove that relationship, and how are we going to self-define? To what are we going to connect ourselves that is bigger than ourselves? Corporations? Causes? Groups? There aren't a lot of other options. None of these are necessarily bad, but here's the reality: none of them are designed to bear the weight of a core design element in our spirit.

When we see someone with an insatiable appetite for the corporate ladder, a ferocious drive for title and reputation, and an addiction to acquisition, we are hovering over the manifestation of a core yearning to believe that there is something bigger than ourselves out there. When we see this infection in a human life, we are viewing someone who is seeking a container larger than themselves in which they can begin to understand themselves and their world. Here is where we can listen and enter spiritual conversations.

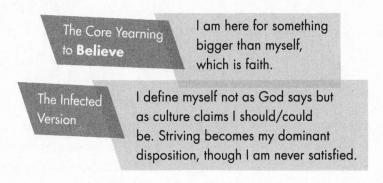

The Core Yearning to **Believe**

I am here for something bigger than myself, which is faith.

The Infected Version

I define myself not as God says but as culture claims I should/could be. Striving becomes my dominant disposition, though I am never satisfied.

To Belong

What about the core yearning to belong and experience unconditional love and acceptance—to be loved and valued for who we are, not just for what we can do? This is the craving for community. Where do we see this head off the path? When we force relationships to carry the burden of defining whether or not we feel accepted, we are heading for trouble. The problem, of course, is that we place all sorts of unspoken expectations on people that, if not met, lead us to feel unwanted, invalidated, and unloved—which often leads to a doubling of effort to get the drive met. This can lead to a raging cycle. The greatest issue here is that so much of our relational behavior is under the surface of our consciousness that we operate, more often than we realize, out of our shadow selves. Driven by underground engines, which once uncovered appear irrational and unrealistic, our shadow selves power a lot of our behavior but remain hidden to our view. It usually doesn't yield a pretty picture.

When we are making demands of others, it is often fueled by the core yearning to belong, but the infected version rears its head and hopes that outside the garden we can create a situation where we feel the unconditional love and acceptance we so desperately crave. The problem is, most people don't feel a need to respond to our demands, nor do they feel they have been placed on the planet to meet our needs. Can you again see how the selfless disposition of Adam and Eve that was traded in for the selfish one is an infection you and I have contracted as well? Can you see how in many relational issues we are hovering over a core yearning for satisfaction? When we see that, we have to learn how to skillfully ask questions that help people realize they are hoping for fulfillment that can really only be found in relationship with God in the garden.

The Core Yearning to **Belong**	I have been created to give and receive unconditional love and acceptance.
The Infected Version	I am unworthy and will never really connect deeply with anyone. I will protect myself and keep people at arm's length, all the while demanding they accept me as I am. Fear is the dominant emotion.

To Become

What about the core yearning to become—the drive to see that
we can have an impact on the future, that we can be something
different tomorrow, that the future can look different from today,
that we can live in hope? This is the craving to help shape tomorrow because we don't want to be stuck in today. As with the
other two, when this core yearning goes careening off the path
of the garden, we end up with addiction, pathology, or dysfunction. We live daily with a hope that we are not at the whim of
"the system," that in some way we aren't trapped and prisoners of
a wicked plot. But we also know that hope for a better tomorrow
can have a dark side. When we constantly focus on tomorrow
and arrive there prematurely anxious about all sorts of details, we
have moved from hope to worry. Wanting a better tomorrow and
yet feeling as though we can't make it happen can lead to anxiety.
Jesus addressed this in Matthew 6:25–34:

> "Therefore I tell you, do not worry about your life, what
> you will eat or drink; or about your body, what you will
> wear. Is not life more important than food, and the body
> more important than clothes? Look at the birds of the air;
> they do not sow or reap or store away in barns, and yet your
> heavenly Father feeds them. Are you not much more valuable
> than they? Can any one of you by worrying add a single hour
> to your life?
>
> "And why do you worry about clothes? See how the flow-
> ers of the field grow. They do not labor or spin. Yet I tell you
> that not even Solomon in all his splendor was dressed like
> one of these. If that is how God clothes the grass of the field,
> which is here today and tomorrow is thrown into the fire,
> will he not much more clothe you—you of little faith? So

do not worry, saying, 'What shall we eat?' or 'What shall we drink?' or 'What shall we wear?' For the pagans run after all these things, and your heavenly Father knows that you need them. But seek first his kingdom and his righteousness, and all these things will be given to you as well. Therefore do not worry about tomorrow, for tomorrow will worry about itself. Each day has enough trouble of its own."

This passage cautions us against living a fragmented existence, which happens every time we project ourselves into the future and fret over what could happen. Hope says tomorrow can be a bright light; worry says it probably won't. Hope says I am a co-creator made in the image of God; worry says no matter what I do, I have deep questions about whether things will turn out all right. Paul gave a prescription to the Philippians for what to do if we find ourselves arriving at the future ahead of schedule:

Do not be anxious about anything, but in every situation, by prayer and petition, with thanksgiving, present your requests to God. And the peace of God, which transcends all understanding, will guard your hearts and your minds in Christ Jesus.

Finally, brothers and sisters, whatever is true, whatever is noble, whatever is right, whatever is pure, whatever is lovely, whatever is admirable—if anything is excellent or praiseworthy—think about such things.

Philippians 4:6–8

Paul's antidote to early arrival at the future is to let our anxiety about it be placed in God's hands and then to focus our mental energy and thoughts on things that bring a sense of lift, delight, beauty, and joy. This sort of mental refocus that moves us from the future back into the present is what Paul says will bring us shalom. The third core yearning has every bit as much potential to derail us as the other two, if we're not careful. Hope's dark side is obsession about tomorrow, with the result that we feel helpless to make a difference.

The Core Yearning to Become

I can become something more tomorrow because I am a cocreator with God. I can do this through hope.

The Infected Version

I can't really make an impact on anything. I am helpless to make a difference, and so I resign myself to my fate. Since I am having little impact, I will power up to manipulate and control, fret and be anxious. Resignation or manipulative drive are the dominant dispositions.

CHAPTER 11

Spiritual Cartography

I love the Maps function on my iPhone. Maps not only has a built-in "find my current location" button, but it can chart the course to my destination, giving me step-by-step instructions. The top of the screen will read, "1 of 12. Turn left on I-94 33.6 miles," and when I hit a button, "2 of 12. Exit 107 Merge right onto ramp .1 miles." The directions make it easy; they are incremental and directional. I'm thankful that someone decided to take this task of cartography and computerize and digitize it so I can have all the benefits of a written map with none of the paper.

We need a spiritual cartography for the conversations we are engaging in. We need to be *incremental* and *directional* as we engage people in the story of their lives and its intersection with God's big story.

In the old modern world, our goal was "close the deal," "finalize the sale," make sure that before they leave they have assurance that if they were to die tonight, they would go to heaven. Since this approach didn't seem to be that of Jesus, Paul, or anyone else in the New Testament, it probably isn't the best one for helping someone consider the path of Jesus.

Just as the furniture salesman who hounds us to death is sure to drive us out of the store, so this type of evangelism is prone to turn off the very people we are trying to invite into conversation and into the journey. I am afraid our goals are sometimes too ambitious and aggressive. Since I can't actually convert anyone and don't have the power to change a human heart, I can relax the sales tactics and just be gentle. This is the admonition of Peter, right? He says we must use "gentleness and respect" as we tell people why we believe.[1]

In spiritual conversations we are inviting people to reorient their lives. We are trying to help those we talk with to find due north and to take some steps in that direction. All of us have a compass that points the way for our lives. All of us have certain maps that help us find our way. In spiritual conversations we are suggesting to people that the dominant maps used to guide and direct their lives are heading them in a disappointing direction. Initial steps toward reorientation on a new map is our hope.

I am convinced that one of the things we must do in spiritual conversations is allow people the freedom to explore and discover the greater viability of new spiritual maps. Telling people that they are wrong, heading to hell, or disgusting in God's eyes simply doesn't give people the chance to explore the potential of the alternative. Our goal is to help establish the possibility of a new direction.

A New Direction

A new direction can mean so much. Take travel, for example. A new direction means new terrain, a change in clothing, weather changes, and different scenery. In other words, reorientation means that everything will change when I fully embrace the new directional heading. This is the fullest meaning of conversion and repentance. Conversion is the process of reorienting and reshaping your life around God's story and the lordship of Jesus. *Reorienting* speaks to a redirectioning; *reshaping* speaks to the indelible marking of a life once the direction has changed.

Conversion, then, has both *directional* and *incremental* components. The directional part may be clear, but what about the incremental part? I think it is quite clear that conversion is a multistage thing. We could say we go through concentric circles of conversion. Red flags popping up in your mind? Bear with me a minute. I thought so, too, the first time I considered this idea.

When we begin to reorient our lives — and for some, it is a conscious moment, while for many others, it is a process that comes with a slower dawning — most of us do so as fully as we can at that moment in time. We surrendered and redirectioned everything we could at that moment in time. We did all we could to use the new map. But something happens as we take another step down this newly reoriented path on the new map we are looking at. We realize that more reorientation of a larger, more encompassing circle of our life is needed. As we travel down this new path and learn new things and explore motives, attitudes, and our views of other people, we realize that our conversion is in some way incomplete. We need to reorient the attitudes in a new direction. We need our motives aligned to this new heading. We recognize quite quickly that this reshaping of our life around God's story and the lordship of Jesus is going to be a long-term project — uh, yeah, a lifetime project. Our life is being reshaped by a different story, by a brand-new narrative. The map is entirely new.

Look at the disciples and you'll realize that they were in a constant reorientation conversation with Jesus. Sometimes they "got it"; sometimes they didn't. It is surprising to see how often they didn't get it when they had the gift of walking with him in real time, in flesh and blood. (I suppose we could be heartened when we realize how often we don't get it either.) But what is clear is that growth came through the reorientation and reshaping of their lives—the same way it happens for us. This reorienting process was not and still is not a onetime deal; it is a daily, ongoing process.

Chad's Narrative Tension

Chad was in an executive team meeting but was texting me on his BlackBerry: *would luv 2 retrn to r conversation at comn gril.*

The summary of the texting flurry amounted to his desire to revisit a topic we had talked about some time ago when we had dinner at the Common Grill. It was the conversation about his journey. This time the conversation would be in a little different setting. He had an "in" with a sweet golf course up in northern Michigan. If I was willing to do overnighters, we could have three days of golf, food, and accommodations—provided!

Chad and I had never done an overnight golf trip. But as I read his text, I was thinking, "Uh, I think I can do an overnighter for free golf, food, and accommodations."

Chad had all the details ironed out, and we were soon going to be on our way for a weekend of resort golf.

He pulled into my driveway and jumped out of his car, sporting a big grin. "Can you believe the weekend weather we're getting? And where we get to be?"

I was grinning too. "Bro, you are the man! I have to hand it to you on this one. You are really bringing the goods to the party." Chad was well connected and loved the perks that accompanied those connections. And I had been the recipient of said perks on more than a few occasions.

We jumped in his car and headed north toward what is one of the prettiest parts of Michigan. As we hit the expressway only a half a mile from my house, Chad was already spouting philosophy. "I've been thinking about the story question you asked me, and I really want to talk about it some more. As I've reflected on the whole story idea, I've really come to wonder what the point of my story is—where it's heading, what I'm really being shaped by. While I'm quite sure I'm writing the story, I'm equally sure I don't know where I, the author, am pointing the plot. In other words, I'm really not sure where I'm headed or what the actual point is."

Chad had to slow down as a deer jumped into the road and bounded to the other side.

"I guess after you asked me about my story," Chad said, "it got me quite literally thinking about 'story,' and I realized I'm really unsure of what the whole point of the life story in general is and what the point of my life story is in particular. Even with all of our God discussion and philosophy stuff, I'm really not sure I can acknowledge the party line of 'God gives my life purpose and meaning.' I know that in some ways it's the expected or correct answer, but I'm just not sure that it's honestly where my story is."

We drove in silence for what seemed like several minutes. Chad looked miserable.

"Chad," I said, "I wasn't asking you to probe the depths of the actual structure of your themes and subplots, but I will say there is something important about that probing, searching, and exploration that just might bring about some real fruit."

"Well, that's what I want to explore a bit this weekend. If I'm honest, I think a good deal of my story is simply being written by the currents of whatever happens. On one hand, I realize I shape a lot of it by the day-to-day actions I engage in. On the other hand, I'm realizing that a lot of what happens just happens; and I'm just not always sure of the rhyme and reason of it all."

I was grinning, and Chad knew why. He interrupted his stream-of-consciousness flow. "Dude! Don't do that to me."

"Chadster! I'm not doing a thing. I'm just listening."

"Listening, my foot! You're thinking I'm somehow seeing the light finally or something like that." Chad said it like he thought he had given away some ground.

I looked at him and shook my head. "Not at all! I've thought a lot about the story and narrative shape of *my* life and of human life in general, and I'm smiling because you are entering into a real wrestling zone that I think is so interesting and fruitful. I remember the first time I entered into this conversation in my head—and it has happened many times since. I'm in the same boat still. I realize that my boat may already be heading out to sea, but I *am* in the same boat."

He interrupted me, narrowed his eyes, and asked, "You really think you're in the same boat?"

"People have sometimes accused me of having it all figured out, but when I say I don't, I really mean I am exploring just like other people are. I admit there are certain pieces and places in my journey I've learned from and have no problem sharing, but I'm not playing games with false humility. There's still an awful lot I haven't figured out."

Chad let out a guttural exclamation. "*Intriguing* is the word that comes to mind, I guess. It's as if you're always on the journey but never really arriving—or at least not ever fully arriving in this life."

"I think the most important part of what you said is, 'A lot of what happens just happens.' That's terribly important to realize. But 'just happens' means that there appear to be hidden forces that just move things along and so we arrive somewhere in our story without really knowing how we got there."

Chad said, "You are going to say that it's always God at work and that I need to tune into that, aren't you? The 'what happens just happens' line is going to haunt me, isn't it, Ron?"

"Actually, you misread me on that one. I wasn't ready to jump to the God part yet, although there is a sense in which God *is* always aware of everything that's going on. Good point."

I grinned at him, and he grudgingly grinned back.

"I was just going to ask what it is that is moving us along in the story," I said. "What is the momentum behind the 'what happens just happens' stuff?"

Chad tilted his head, grabbed his sunglasses from the visor, and said, "Good question. And honestly, I haven't thought about it a ton."

"I bet you've thought about it more than you realize. You and I have talked about your thrill in being part of the corporate hunt, your love of the tech toys, the life you get to live. What do you think drives all that? Were you just born with it? Is it a conscious decision to pursue it? Fate working itself out? Or is it something more subtle and yet perhaps more powerful?" I reached around to the backseat and grabbed a can of cashews and popped off the top.

"You know, Ron," Chad said, "one of the more interesting things that has happened in our conversations is I've had to start asking hard questions about myself, about stuff going on in me. I feel far more comfortable talking about things we were talking about at the beginning—things such as Karen Armstrong, or

Moby blogs, or philosophy and epistemology. This 'probing my inner life' stuff is hard."

"Buddy, that is the journey, though, isn't it?" I asked. "When we keep everything theoretical and distant, it's easy to keep this at arm's length. But when we start moving into how this impacts us—our trajectory, our story, our directional heading, then we're starting to ask big questions."

We began to hit a portion of the expressway where you see nothing but green, lush trees and scenic beauty. It was a perfect weekend to travel to northern Michigan.

"What do you sense going on inside you, then, with these questions you're asking yourself?" I queried.

"You know, I'm confident of myself, and pretty content. But I have to say, these questions are unsettling and almost make me want to ignore them."

"Why are they unsettling?" I asked.

"I think I have everything pretty well together. I keep all this philosophy stuff in my head because it keeps me thinking about interesting things. But then when I have to probe much deeper, I wonder if I have as much figured out as I think I do."

"So you think the goal is to figure it out," I replied, "whatever 'it' may be?"

"I'm not so sure that's my goal, but I think there is this pressure to have life figured out, to love your job, or at least to do well at it, to have the sort of rewards that doing well affords—you know all that stuff of the American Dream. So in many ways I *do* have it all figured out. I *am* living the American Dream at some level, and life is good. But the more I ask these questions you put in my head, the more uncertain I am that I have it all figured out. I think the most challenging thing I've thought about in a while is this whole 'story' conversation that started at The Common Grill."

Chad pulled off the interstate for some coffee and said to me, "I know. I won't even ask. No coffee for you, just blue label Lo-Carb Monster." Chad looked at me, rolling his eyes like I was some sort of teenager who hadn't graduated to real adult drinks like coffee yet.

"That's right, but I'll go in with you. I may be tapping their Krispy Kreme reserves." Chad smiled, and we headed into the convenience store, got our food and drink, and jumped back in the car and onto the expressway.

Chad looked at me and said, "Where were we in the conversation?"

"You were saying that The Common Grill conversation about your story was disconcerting, or something like that."

"Oh, yeah, that's right," Chad said, nodding as he reconnected his train of thought. "I don't like to think too deeply about this because I realize that my intellectualizing may be my way of keeping tension at bay."

"OK, that's interesting," I said. "Tension about what?"

"I think I have a lot of this figured out, but when I ask myself what exactly I've figured out, there isn't much there. I've thought about all sorts of ideas. I've explored a ton of little concepts, but nothing really that is what I could call a story. In fact, for all the ideas and concepts, you would think I have the meaning and purpose of life figured out." Chad's voice and demeanor had gotten somewhat sarcastic as he admitted he really didn't have it all nailed down. "And there is the tension. My life isn't as purposeful or cohesive or, uh—I don't know the word I'm looking for, but my life doesn't seem nearly as deep as I thought it was."

"And that is a problem in some way?" I asked.

"Not a problem, I guess, but I do know this: Life should have a sense of purpose and meaning, and I realize that mine seems like it has a very limited and shallow purpose and meaning. When I reflect on my story, I'm not sure who or what I actually live for. In all honesty, I realize that I live for me and for the stuff I want to acquire."

"And that creates tension?" I asked, almost under my breath.

"It seems pretty thin to me. In the privacy of this car ride, I might say it sounds mighty selfish." Chad paused and let his own words sink in. I was silent and pondered them with him.

I broke the silence, "You know the crazy part? The selfishness and thinness never seem to subside. When we use the old 'more of the same' solution in our story we only end up on what I call the never-ending spin of the gerbil wheel."

"Yeah, well, we call it climbing the infinitely long corporate ladder," Chad said. "But I suppose the gerbil wheel is the same idea —ladder and gerbil wheels, both are images of never-ending pursuit and perhaps our lack of brilliance at seeing that both lead nowhere."

I quietly registered my agreement.

Trajectory

I don't know whether Chad could see what was going on in him. We hadn't been on the road more than a couple of hours, and he was already wrestling with life trajectory issues. Granted there had been months of conversations, questions, dinners, and golf rounds to get here, but Chad *was* arriving at this place all in his time and all on the timeline of his discovery journey. This is, in my opinion, exactly what reorientation is all about. The recognition, or maybe I should say the slowly dawning recognition (because I'm not sure he recognized anything yet), that his current directional heading was not very satisfying was reaching the surface of his heart and mind. When we begin to recognize that our life narrative has tensions we opted for either unknowingly or with little forethought, we are on a possible path of reorientation or redirectioning. This is, in fact, what spiritual conversion is all about.

Chad is recognizing the selfishness of his story. It's the very essence of what we identified in the garden as the fundamental infection contracted by Adam and Eve. When the American Dream is the primary tension provider in our story, the thinness Chad is recognizing is bound to eventually occur.

"I guess on this little road trip north I'm coming to some realizations," Chad said as he grabbed the cashew can off the center console and knocked his iPod on the floor. I interrupted him to reach down and grab it. "Way to go, Grace," I teased.

"Excuse me. I'm in the middle of a thought, thank you! I was saying my biggest realization is that the motivations for my personal story aren't so noble. I certainly don't think they are evil or bad, but they aren't in any way good or helpful, or impacting the world at all. And that brings me a sense of sadness." He glanced over at me. "I need to share with you something that happened just this past weekend. I was watching TV, and a special on Darfur came on. Later I saw a documentary on dealing with homelessness in urban America. And it suddenly dawned on me that I really don't do anything to better the world or to help people in the world. For all of my criticism of the church, I realize that I don't do anything either, other than wearing a couple of these rubber bracelets to show my one dollar's worth of support for the cause."

"I wonder if our life purposes have to be huge or grandiose,"

I said. "I think I hear what you're saying when you tell me you don't feel like yours are very noble. But I'd like to hear more about what you're thinking about there. All of us can't have global impact. All of us won't change the world. But we all can put an imprint on our corner of the world or neighborhood or office conference room or classroom."

"I get that," Chad said, nodding slowly. "I guess I tend to feel like if you can't go big, you ought to go home. But you're right. Am I making a dent in the opportunities around me, or am I waiting to bring peace to some remote nation-state?"

I laughed and said, "Yeah, right."

Chad laughed and continued. "As I'm thinking about my life narrative, this all seems like a pretty big 'aha!' experience. Not sure what I'm supposed to do with all this going on inside of me. I rarely feel this churned-up inside."

Chad breathed a slight sigh of relief and called attention to our arrival at the entrance of the golf resort. "Guess I can give my brain *and* my rumbling gut a rest and not think about this stuff for a while at least—because I'm ready to change clothes and hit the driving range."

I looked at him and said, "I just want to note I wasn't the one who suggested the brain-hurting, heart-tugging conversation. That would be, uh—that's right—*you* who suggested that. So any discomfort is your own doing. But don't think I'm not ready to take it back up when you are. I am not afraid! And I sure hope I don't hear some wimpy excuse related to this conversation when I beat you down on the first eighteen holes we play."

Chad laughed and said something about "in my fantasies" and told me we would indeed be resuming our dialogue, but for right now we had to be content to unpack our golf clubs and get ready for a great weekend.

The Message Never Changes,
but Our Understandings Surely Do

In the world of spiritual conversations, things are more organic, real, centered on listening to the narrative of someone's life and the transformational yearnings they are in touch with.

This is difficult for us to hear. I hear with regularity a concern that was voiced yet again in an interview I did on a national radio talk program recently. The interviewer said, "Isn't the concern, though, that in changing the methods, we'll compromise the message we've been telling?" My response to the interviewer was the response I have been giving for some time now: "The very concern about compromising the *message we've been telling* has an underlying assumption that the message we've been telling is the whole, unabbreviated, full message that Jesus came to offer. This is a massive and faulty assumption. One of the big challenges we face as we undergo some of the major shifts the church is facing is to realize that the way we have told the story may not be the whole story."

If our understanding of the message that Jesus brought grows deeper and fuller, and if it better explains the content and detail of the biblical story, then the problem is what? Our goal is far more profound and important than being hard core or uncompromising about past methodology. Our goal is to tell the whole and unabbreviated story as spoken and lived by the One around whom we orient our lives.

When we are hovering over these sorts of ideas related to the life reorientation of a guy like Chad, I would argue that we are at the very crux of what repentance is. Our infection is an orientation of life around a wrong set of values, goals, and hopes. Selfishness is a heart-deep issue. We have hearts that long to do things our way, satisfy our cravings our way, and fill our interior yearnings our way.

On one hand, the image of God in us is the residence of those God-placed, God-designed yearnings. On the other hand, the infection we have leads us down the path of attempting to fulfill these yearnings in ways that are bound to disappoint, essentially because these yearnings were designed to function in a garden context that is without infection.

So we were made in the image of God, but our infected trans-formational architecture has us careening off the path of shalom wholeness. This in turn makes being shalom brokers to others nearly impossible. Selfishness reigns in our infected yearnings. But this is where Jesus comes into the story. He comes as the full-ness of the image of God in bodily form, not a partial or obscured *imago dei*, but the fullness of it. Here is one of the key theological connections between the first and second creations.[2] Jesus is the full image of God, the untainted example of *imago dei* in flesh. In other words, Jesus isn't just *imago dei*; he is uninfected *imago dei*.

Breath/Wind/Spirit

Adam and Eve were breathed into by God—breathed/spirited/winded into being. Their very life existence was created and sustained by the Spirit of God. It is no wonder, then, that when we come to the New Testament, passages such as John 16 call out and remind us of the Spirit's work in the life of every human being on the planet. Not just Christians—everyone! Many Christians just can't wrap their heads around this idea. But the animating Spirit who gives life to every human being is the very same Spirit who convicts, draws, and prompts, according to John's gospel. It is in the same section of John where Jesus declares that the disciples are at an advantage when he leaves because his departure will pave the way for the coming of the Holy Spirit. There will be a person called the Holy Spirit with whom they will have a relationship. Furthermore, it is this Spirit's working deep inside every human being that will be responsible for any reorientation and the promptings that provoke it.

The challenging thing is to recognize that the Spirit of God who animates every human life is the very same Spirit we have a relationship with as a Christ-follower, the same Spirit who places interior promptings in the person who is not yet a follower. Coming to grips with the activity of the Spirit of God within humanity at large may be one of the big areas of investigation and conversation in the years ahead.

I wonder if Amos Yong's thesis is right. He raises the question of what might happen if we were to move the center and locus of evaluation for everything Christian from soteriology and answering the question, "What can get you saved?" to a more pervasive, foundational, and garden/creation-based question, namely, "Where is the Spirit at work?" Yong's thesis proposes that we shift the conversation from soteriology (salvation) as the center to pneumatology (spirit) if we want to have conversations in a religiously plural context.[3]

Restoration

Adam and Eve swapped their selfless cocreative role in the garden for a selfish role of judging. Infection meant a swapping of selfless for selfish and an entering into the judging and separational function that only God, in his infinite wisdom, was to have. In the Incarnation, Jesus comes and addresses both of these issues. He shows how those **made** *imago dei* are to **live** *imago dei*. He models in the healthiest and most functional way possible what it means to cocreatively, selflessly, and restoratively serve the world and those around him—and how to live out what life would have been like in the garden.

Jesus modeled the way for us to see how his restoration program plays out on this earth. Do you remember my earlier statement that if we don't understand creation and the first part of the story, it will be difficult to understand what Jesus came to restore? Well, here we have it. The abbreviated story of fall-redemption never asks the question about the purpose in the original creation because the story starts in Genesis 3—the fall. As such, we don't know what the restoration Jesus is trying to bring is really all about. But when we begin with creation, followed by fall-redemption, we have a clear sense of the last piece of the story —restoration.

Jesus is on a massive restoration mission, which is only to restate what he said in one of his personal mission statement talks in Luke 4 as he read from the Isaiah 61 scroll about the great reversals of the prisoners and the oppressed being set free and the blind receiving sight. In these great reversals we hear echoes of Eden, our original home.

Jesus walks the earth handing out pink spoon samples of the kingdom of God, fulfilling the great reversal passages of the prophet Isaiah[4] and teaching the disciples to pursue the same mission. He teaches them to pray that the kingdom, rule, reign, will, and life of God would come to this earth and be here, just as it is in heaven.[5] Much of what Jesus does is to bring tastes of garden restoration, and he models for the disciples how they can do the same.

Alternative Story Line

To use the narrative language we've explored throughout the book, Jesus provides an alternative story line, an alternative plot tension. We can either live the American Dream, with all of its bait-and-switch frustrations, or we can opt to reorient our lives around a different plot tension and story line in which we are part of Jesus' restoration team on this earth. The two stories are quite literally worlds apart and tap our transformational architecture in entirely different ways. One story promises adrenaline, posing as a momentary rush of happiness; the other story offers selfless service as the route to shalom.

In short, Jesus provides the example of *imago dei* in the flesh, so to speak—an example that Adam and Eve had been commissioned to provide and should have provided. In this way, Jesus is indeed a second Adam. This is the great invitation, the great reorientation. We are invited to be a part of the great restoration team of Jesus, addressing brokenness, difficult relationships, physical distress, dysfunctional cycles, addictive patterns—and the list goes on. That is what it means to follow Jesus—heading out to offer pink spoons all around in order to see who wants the whole scoop.

This selfless modeling is graphically illustrated in the way Jesus took on the most toxic and selfish manifestations of the infection—as seen in the unrelenting judgmentalism of the religious leaders of his day. Jesus meets these leaders head-on, and the primary issue always comes down to *judging*—who lives up to the law, who is in and who is out, who is acceptable and who is not. Very few conflicts—I'm not sure I can think of any—are about anything else but judging. And if we're careful, perhaps we can be honest enough to examine how our churches are doing in this area. And remember, this isn't taking potshots. It's learning to be

■ 221

critical thinkers and to do all we can to avoid ending up being just like the Pharisees.

So Jesus not only provides a flesh-and-blood example of what it means to selflessly serve and to model the restoration he invites all of us into; he not only takes on the religious establishment so deeply infected with judgment. He comes to deal with the infection so we can overcome its overwhelming gravitational pull on our spirits. Jesus' death, burial, and resurrection demonstrate that he is the king and worthy of the full reorientation of our lives. His life modeled selfless serving; his shedding of his blood in death makes it possible for us to follow in his footsteps by giving us the antidote for our infection.

But like all infections, healing isn't instantaneous. There is a gravitational pull toward the selfish. When you look at all the failures, foibles, and flubs we get caught in, almost all of them have at their root some selfish proclivity, some self-centered drive, some egocentric expression. Jesus' incarnation modeled the way out of that gravitational pull, and his death showed the ultimate selfless example, paying a price for our selfishness and thereby making a way to connect to him in intimate personal relationship. In this personal relationship, we can allow him to live in and through us, thus making the ego in us less and less. In short, as ego dies, the real *imago dei* emerges. As the "Ron" defined by all sorts of external trappings is put to death, the infection loses its power and is increasingly minimized, and the Jesus in me can live fully. Isn't this exactly what Paul meant in his words to the Galatians?

> I have been crucified with Christ and I no longer live, but Christ lives in me. The life I now live in the body, I live by faith in the Son of God, who loved me and gave himself for me.
>
> Galatians 2:20

This is the very reason the body of Christ metaphor works in Paul's writings. For where ego is dying in you and me and her and him, there is the emergence of Jesus in you and me and her and him. This means that where ego dies and *imago dei* lives, I am just like you. This is where Paul's theology of the body is so important. In a world divided by factions, strife, political maneuverings, famine, AIDS, and so on, it is *imago dei* in us that forms our core likeness with each other, as members of the same body.

Paul also gives evidence of the loosening influence of this infection when he writes of the fruit of the Spirit.[6] And notice that fruit is always expressed, seen, visible. The very metaphor of fruit implies process and progress. The full reorientation of our lives is an ongoing, lifelong, and challenging pursuit. The proof of reorientation is an increasing amount of fruit. This is such an important point. A fully reoriented life isn't marked by a more spiritual to-do list. Our spiritual formation isn't illustrated by how much of the Bible we read or can recite, how much money we give, or how many hours we serve in the church. All of these tasks can be done with hearts far from King Jesus. No, says Paul. Fruit such as love, joy, peace, patience, and kindness — these are the kinds of virtues that indicate reorientation.

Ongoing Conversation

Bearing this fruit will require a new awareness level and an experiential instead of informational spiritual formation model that takes this awareness seriously. In the past, most spiritual formation models have been textual. In other words, they've been about interaction with the biblical text and other texts and about studying, memorizing, and meditating on the text. This doesn't mean that nontextual patterns and practices have been absent, but they've clearly been in the background. This informational view of discipleship is undergoing and will continue to undergo a radical reshaping to a spiritual formation model with a greater emphasis on awareness—something that resembles the spiritual formation of the pre-Gutenberg days. We take to heart what Jesus said: "I love the Father and do exactly what my Father has commanded me."[7]

As our ongoing spiritual formation, or conversion, becomes increasingly awareness and experience based, and as we move from spiritual formation as information transmission to models and indicators geared to producing fruit, we will find life change at the core of those who reorient their lives around Jesus. God's transformational architecture will then produce in us just what God had designed and hoped for when the garden project began.

Spiritual conversations can happen when we personally understand the ongoing process of *letting go* of a life narrative shaped by the relentless spin of the gerbil wheel and instead *continually reorient* our lives around a larger, more compelling narrative. When we are in process, continually in touch with the deep transformational yearnings we've been designed with, we find we have new ears. We have new sensitivities to listen to our friends and family. We have ears for the telltale signs that transformational yearnings are seeking satisfaction outside the garden in dysfunctional and infected ways. It is a path and story with which we are deeply familiar in our own lives and can therefore listen patiently and join the journey with others who are exploring the path. We notice the hints and clues when we are hovering over *imago dei* and the three longings with which God inspirited all of us at birth.

What could be more important?

Back to Chad

Chad and I had just played a great round of golf, with not much conversation about anything except our golf game, which actually helped us play better—at least it helped me play better! We were in the parking lot, loading clubs into the trunk, when Chad dropped a bit of a bomb. I suddenly realized why we hadn't been chewing over our typical twilight topics of conversation.

"Ron, before we go, I have some news. Actually some pretty great news. The company is transferring me to Seattle. I am so darn pumped. Great city—and a 22 percent pay increase!"

"You're kidding me, right?"

"Nope, buddy. Dead serious. They're moving the sales operation there, and I can either move or go look for a new job. They're paying for the move, of course—but they can't pay for the friendships I'll have to leave behind. That's the part I'm not looking forward to."

"Chad, I'm happy for you. Great to hear they want you to go with them. You could have just lost your job. But let me say, I'm bummed for me. I've totally enjoyed our twilight connection and winter workouts. Especially the conversation. It has been great! So when is all this coming down?"

"I have to move in two weeks. They're packing up my house and moving me to a condo until I find a house I like. But that isn't what I really wanted to tell you. When I knew I was going to talk to you about this, I was overwhelmed deep inside by what has happened over these many months. I'm not sure I'd ever really been in touch with how profound the changes are that are going on inside me.

"Ron, I need to tell you something. This spiritual process I'm involved in, the journey I'm on—well, it's been, I guess it's fair to say, life changing. I'll be honest. We've talked about things during a golf round that roll around in me for weeks. I really feel like I've taken some steps forward into new terrain. I don't think I have it all figured out, but I do think I have a grasp of the Christian story I've never had before."

"Chad, you need to know that the last year and a half has been incredible for me too. I've learned so much from you and have examined my own journey in the process. We've definitely had some challenging conversations, haven't we?"

"Let's go get a bite to eat, Ron. We don't have to stand here and act like it's the last time we'll ever talk. Email and weekend golf trips will just have to be in the future and—who knows?—maybe there's more spiritual conversations to be had."

Journey (Still) in Progress

Chad and I still email and chat on Skype and on cell phones, and we've seen each other a couple of times since he moved. Chad has found a learning community where he continues his spiritual quest. Sounds like a church small group type of thing. He tells me he periodically checks out a church he has heard is good, but he never seems to land there. But it is exciting. He is growing. He is reading and asking questions and seemingly drawing closer to God. He talks about praying and about learning about the life of Jesus and about what's going on with his character development. He is even spearheading the Extreme Home Makeover project in the Seattle area to help twelve families with new home construction.

Where exactly is he in the journey? I'm not sure. But I can barely answer that question about myself half the time. All I know is that it sounds as though he's making every effort to take steps in the right direction. And when he talks about his story? Well, that also sounds as though it is being reshaped by much larger considerations. As I recall conversations from two years ago and compare them to the cell phone conversation I had with him the other day, something has surely happened, and it sounds as though his life is being reshaped. How exciting is that?!

Notes

Introduction: Transformational Architecture

1. Robert E. Quinn, *Deep Change: Discovering the Leader Within* (San Francisco: Jossey-Bass, 1996), 15–28.

2. See Joshua 10:12–13.

Chapter 1: The Context

1. Moby, "Religion," Journal Archive, August 2005, http://www.moby.com/journal/archive/200508.

2. University of Notre Dame, "Latin Dictionary and Grammar Aid," http://catholic.archives.nd.edu/cgi-bin/lookup.pl?stem=cultus&ending=.

3. For the trivialization of God and relegating him to the margins, see the well-written (if at times too simple) *The Trivialization of God: The Dangerous Illusion of a Manageable Deity* by Donald McCullough (Colorado Springs: NavPress, 1995).

4. Willis Harman, *Global Mind Change: The Promise of the 21st Century*, 2d ed. (San Francisco: Berrett-Koehler, 1998), 33.

5. Quoted in David M. Harrison, "Bell's Theorem," http://www.upscale.utoronto.ca/PVB/Harrison/BellsTheorem/BellsTheorem.html.

6. David Bohm, *Wholeness and the Implicate Order* (New York: Routledge, 1980).

7. For an overview of the cool rationalism of the modern world that is dying out, see Stephen Toulmin, *Cosmopolis: The Hidden Agenda of Modernity* (Chicago: University of Chicago Press, 1990).

8. See Jacques Derrida, "Faith and Knowledge: The Two Sources of Religion

at the Limits of Mere Reason" in *Religion*, ed. Jacques Derrida and Gianni Vattimo (Palo Alto, Calif.: Stanford University Press, 1998), 1–78.

9. Ibid, 56.

10. Rick Warren, *The Purpose Driven Life* (Grand Rapids: Zondervan, 2002).

11. Witness the revealnow.com website posted by Willow Creek Community Church, South Barrington, Illinois, as an example.

12. Kevin Vanhoozer, *The Drama of Doctrine* (Louisville: Westminster, 2005), 266.

13. Nancy Gibbs, "The Good Samaritans," *Time* magazine, December 19, 2005.

14. See "Copenhagen Consensus," http://www.copenhagenconsensus.com; "UN Millennium Development Goals," http://www.un.org/millenniumgoals.

15. See "Copenhagen Consensus 2006: A United Nations Perspective," http://www.copenhagenconsensus.com/Default.aspx?ID=158.

16. David Korten, *The Great Turning* (San Francisco: Berrett-Koehler, 2006).

17. George Barna, *Revolution* (Wheaton, Ill.: Tyndale, 2005), 31–32.

18. See Karen Armstrong, *The Great Transformation* (New York: Knopf, 2006); see also her *A History of God* (New York: Knopf, 1993).

19. See Jessica Roemischer, "A New Axial Age: Karen Armstrong on the History—and the Future—of God," *What Is Enlightenment?* magazine (December 2005–February 2006), http://www.wie.org/j31/armstrong.asp?pf=1.

Chapter 2: The Biblical Text

1. The work of Gerhard Hasel (*Old Testament Theology: Basic Issues in the Current Debate* [Grand Rapids: Eerdmans, 1991]) on the search for an Old Testament *Mitte*, or central unifying theme, is a good summary of the conversation. Marcus Borg (*The Heart of Christianity* [New York: HarperOne, 2004]) is the first person I've seen who has identified these three narratives as framing stories.

2. Luke 19:45–48.

3. For a bite-size nugget on this topic, see the Answers.com entry, http://www.answers.com/topic/karen-armstrong. For a more sophisticated and detailed treatment, see Karen Armstrong, *The Battle for God* (New York: Knopf, 2000).

4. See Acts 1:6; 3:19–21; Colossians 1:19–20.

5. James McClendon, *Doctrine: Systematic Theology*, vol. 2 (Nashville: Abingdon, 1994), 230–31.

6. For the best treatment, albeit massive and complex, that takes into consideration a host of postmodern issues regarding meaning in a text, see Kevin Vanhoozer, *Is There a Meaning in This Text?* (Grand Rapids: Zondervan, 1998).

7. Jean-François Lyotard, *The Postmodern Condition: A Report on Knowledge* (Manchester: Manchester University Press, 1984), xxiv.

8. While there are a stack of resources on this topic ranging from academic philosophy to literary theory written by those sympathetic to a Christian worldview, I think the best bang for your one-volume buck on the narrative story is Gerard Loughlin, *Telling God's Story: Bible, Church and Narrative Theology* (Cambridge: Cambridge University Press, 1996). Written some fifteen years earlier, but powerful in its narrative depiction of the biblical story, is George Stroup, *The Promise of Narrative Theology: Recovering the Gospel in the Church* (Eugene, Ore.: Wipf and Stock, 1981). The classic books dealing with narrative methodology are Robert Alter, *The Art of Biblical Narrative* (New York: Basic Books, 1983), and Hans W. Frei, *The Eclipse of Biblical Narrative* (New Haven, Conn.: Yale University Press, 1980).

Chapter 3: The Human Text

1. Thomas H. Davenport and John C. Beck, *The Attention Economy* (Cambridge, Mass.: Harvard Business School Press, 2001).

2. Zygmunt Bauman, *Liquid Times* (Cambridge: Polity Press, 2007), 3.

Chapter 4: *Imago Dei*

1. For a full-scale treatment and persuasive account of the royal court image, see the first two chapters in J. Richard Middleton, *The Liberating Image* (Grand Rapids: Brazos, 2005).

2. For a good summary of the options, see Stanley Grenz, *The Social God and the Relational Self: A Trinitarian Theology of the* Imago Dei (Louisville: Westminster, 2001), esp. 183–222.

3. Middleton, *Liberating Image*, 27.

4. Ibid., 26.

5. I realize I'm painting a composite view when I use the phrase "creation stories." These all have unique features and deserve study in their own right, but for our purposes I simply want to show that the image of God as articulated in Genesis is in fact a significant point of departure from other creation accounts and that this point of departure is significant for spiritual conversations and for our inviting people into God's story.

6. Remember that these are not archaeological treatises or medical or scientific documents—but stories.

7. See Middleton, *Liberating Image*, 210.

8. This forbidding is recorded much later in the Bible text, admittedly, at Exodus 20.

9. See Psalm 8 for another reminder of how humanity is the crowning glory of God's creation. Psalm 8 has been acknowledged by many Old Testament scholars and Psalms experts as a commentary, or picture of sorts, on Genesis 1 and the image of God in humanity.

10. See Genesis 2:19–20.

11. Middleton, *Liberating Image*, 211.

12. Ibid., 217.

13. See the dialogue between Ken Wilber and Father Thomas Keating at an Integral Christianity conference in Denver, Colorado (April 24, 2006), http://in.integralinstitute.org/live/view_frthomas2.aspx. The same material can be found in Ken Wilber, *Integral Spirituality* (Boston: Shambhala, 2006), 18–22, 40–42. The application of this 1P, 2P, 3P language to God is most fully developed in Ken Wilber, *The One, Two, Three of God* audiobook (audio CD; Louisville, Colo.: Sounds True, 2006).

Chapter 5: You and Me — Gods?

1. See 1 Corinthians 3:9; 2 Corinthians 5:20; 6:1.

2. I have noted that the metaphors surrounding this sort of atonement story are "legal," "judicial," "judge," "justice," and so on—but a different storying would lead to a different set of metaphors that may prove far more connective and just as faithful to the biblical story.

3. Though I'm certainly not suggesting that this is a primary or catalytic reason for the division between East and West, I will leave it to church historians, which I am not, to help us fully understand the issues surrounding what is called the Great Schism of AD 1023.

4. C. S. Lewis, *God in the Dock* (Grand Rapids: Eerdmans, 1970), 112.

5. C. S. Lewis, *Mere Christianity* (New York: Macmillan, 1952), 174.

6. For a great anthology of articles on *theosis* or *divinization*, see Michael Christensen and Jeffery Wittung, eds., *Partakers of the Divine Nature: The History and Development of Deification in the Christian Traditions* (Grand Rapids: Baker, 2008). The articles on *theosis* in Martin Luther and John Calvin will be of particular interest for Protestants. These articles help show this isn't a distinctly Eastern church conversation.

7. For an online article that will help fill in some details for those who are new to this idea, see Wikipedia, http://en.wikipedia.org/wiki/Theosis.

8. See 1 John 4:8, 16.

9. Hans Urs von Balthasar, *Love Alone Is Credible* (Fort Collins, Colo.: Ignatius, 2005), 70.

Chapter 6: The Infectious Judger Gene

1. Spiritual Explorations Live (SEL) is now a web-based community where we do live webcasting with full chat capability. For more information, visit www.velocityculture.com and click on the Spiritual Explorations icon.

2. See Genesis 3:5.

3. 1 Corinthians 13:12 KJV.

4. While there are many passages in the Gospels on this topic, you can begin by looking at the Pharisees' challenge to Jesus about the right people to eat with (Mark 2:13–17). Note, too, Jesus' redefinition of family in Mark 3:31–35 (graphically illustrated by those standing outside the house and those seated around him inside the house). Matthew 7:1–2 (see also Luke 6:37) records Jesus' command against judging. Jesus is careful to say that when he judges, he doesn't do so alone but in keeping with what he sees in the Father (John 5:30; 8:15–18). For a great book on this topic, see Gregory A. Boyd, *Repenting of Religion* (Grand Rapids: Baker, 2004).

5. A study by David Kinnaman (*UnChristian* [Grand Rapids: Baker, 2007]) says that 87 percent of those age sixteen to twenty-nine polled said that the church was judgmental—second only to those who said that the church was antigay (91 percent).

6. See Matthew 9:12.

7. See John 8:2–11.

8. Genesis 5:1. The same thing is reiterated postflood in Genesis 9:6.

9. Ken Wilber, *No Boundaries* (Boston: Shambhala, 2001).

10. See 1 Corinthians 12:26.

11. Frederica Mathewes-Green, "Thoughts on Haggard," *First Things* (November 7, 2006), http://www.firstthings.com/onthesquare/?p=520.

12. The infection doesn't always overwhelm, of course. I'm sure all of us can think of plenty of people who claim no connection to God and who do plenty of benevolent things—simply due to the *imago dei*.

Chapter 7: Fresh Infusion

1. These are all English translations of the same Hebrew word *rûah* in the Old Testament.

2. See Amos Yong, *Beyond the Impasse* (Grand Rapids: Baker, 2003) for a

pneumatic understanding of how God works in humans and human institutions. His thesis is elegant and powerful, with far-reaching implications for what we think is going on in human experience.

3. Same English translation for both the Greek word *pneuma* and the Hebrew word *rûaḥ*.

4. See especially John 3 and Acts 2.

5. Think of Paul and his speech in Athens (Acts 17:22–31) as an example.

6. In addition to doing a Google search on "Nike" and "evangelist," check out www.robfrankel.com, where "the best branding expert on the planet" describes his job as turning product users into evangelists for your brand.

Chapter 8: Our Lost Story Chapters

1. See Michael White and David Epston, *Narrative Means to Therapeutic Ends* (New York: Norton, 1990).

2. Scot McKnight, *Turning to Jesus* (Louisville: Westminster, 2002), 4.

3. Ibid., 13.

Chapter 9: New Vantage Points

1. For a detailed look at these types of knowledge, though using different nomenclature, and their relationship to truth, beauty, and goodness, see Ken Wilber, *The Marriage of Sense and Soul* (New York: Broadway, 1998), 49–58.

2. For treatments of these waves of epochs and insights into key intellectual markers of those eras, see Bill Bryson, *A Short History of Nearly Everything* (New York: Broadway, 2003); see also Anthony Gottlieb, *The Dream of Reason* (New York: W.W. Norton, 2000).

3. Morris Berman, *Coming to Our Senses: Body and Spirit in the Hidden History of the West* (New York: Simon & Schuster, 1989).

4. For a great treatment on how the intuition is processing underneath our conscious and often buzzing mind see Guy Claxton, *Hare Brain and Tortoise Mind* (New York: HarperCollins, 1999).

5. Numerous figures could be noted who have helped with these advances. But one of the most important futurists and inventors of our time, with all the awards and patents to prove it, is Ray Kurzweil (see his *The Age of Spiritual Machines* [New York: Penguin, 2000] and his magisterial recent work *The Singularity Is Near* [New York: Penguin, 2006]).

6. Josh McDowell's *Evidence That Demands a Verdict* (San Bernardino, Calif.: Here's Life, 1972) was the quintessential modernist handbook to evangelism and

apologetics. The revised volume, *More Evidence That Demands a Verdict* (San Bernardino, Calif.: Here's Life, 1981), and the follow-up book *New Evidence That Demands a Verdict* (Nashville: Nelson, 1999), were, well—more of the same. In no way would I say that these books weren't helpful and didn't serve an important purpose. But we have to be fair in observing that all historically situated or constructed material and tools will eventually have to be shelved or revised because culture is a container constantly morphing its shape.

7. Do an Amazon.com search for "spirit" or "soul," and notice how many books have been published in the last ten to fifteen years on this topic. It is amazingly situational.

8. For a brilliant treatment on how we really know what we know and some the pitfalls of the "objective knowledge is superior to subjective knowledge" theses of the modern world, see Michael Polanyi, *Personal Knowledge* (Chicago: University of Chicago Press, 1974). You will have to do some hard thinking as you read, but the benefits are worth it. For the implications of knowledge shifts for discipleship, see Lesslie Newbigin, *Proper Confidence: Faith, Doubt, and Certainty in Christian Discipleship* (Grand Rapids: Eerdmans, 1995).

Chapter 10: Yearnings for Wholeness

1. Christopher Lasch, *The Culture of Narcissism*, rev. ed. (New York: W. W. Norton, 1991).

2. See Isaiah 51 and Ezekiel 36.

3. Genesis 2:18.

4. Ellen Dissanayake, *Homo Aestheticus* (Seattle: University of Washington Press, 1995), 39–63.

5. Ephesians 2:10.

6. Jeremiah 18:4.

7. Roberta Gilbert, *Extraordinary Relationships: A New Way of Thinking About Human Interaction* (New York: Wiley, 1992), 12.

8. For two of the best books about this from a Christian community perspective, see Joe Myers, *The Search to Belong* (Grand Rapids: Zondervan, 2003), and his *Organic Community* (Grand Rapids: Baker, 2007).

9. This makes me think of Paul's prayer for the Ephesians: "I pray that you, being rooted and established in love, may have power, together with all the Lord's people, to grasp how wide and long and high and deep is the love of Christ, and to know this love that surpasses knowledge—that you may be filled to the measure of all the fullness of God" (Ephesians 3:17–19). Paul knew there was something deeply maturing about the connective love of God that gives us freedom as we

surrender ourselves to be who he has made us to be, no matter what anyone else thinks. It is hard to think of anything that could be more liberating.

10. See such passages as Romans 12:1–2 and Philippians 2:12–13 for an example of what I'm talking about.

11. See 1 John 4:7–8, 16.

12. Mihaly Csikszentmihalyi, *Good Business; Leadership, Flow, and the Making of Meaning* (New York: Viking, 2003), 28–29.

13. See ibid., 29.

14. Ibid., 6.

15. Ibid., 7.

16. Genesis 3:17.

Chapter 11: Spiritual Cartography

1. 1 Peter 3:15.

2. See Colossians 1:15–20.

3. See Amos Yong, *Beyond the Impasse* (Grand Rapids: Baker, 2003).

4. See Isaiah 29; 35; 42; 52–53; 61.

5. See the Lord's Prayer in Matthew 6.

6. See Galatians 5:22–23.

7. John 14:31.